Q 2372

P9-DMO-809

EDUCATION

Opposing Viewpoints®

Mary E. Williams, *Book Editor*

Bruce Glassman, *Vice President*
Bonnie Szumski, *Publisher*
Helen Cothran, *Managing Editor*

OPPOSING
VIEWPOINTS®
SERIES

GREENHAVEN PRESS

An imprint of Thomson Gale, a part of The Thomson Corporation

THOMSON
————✳————™
GALE

Detroit • New York • San Francisco • San Diego • New Haven, Conn.
Waterville, Maine • London • Munich

LIBRARY OF CONGRESS CATALOGING-IN-PUBLICATION DATA

Education : opposing viewpoints / Mary E. Williams, book editor.
    p. cm. — (Opposing viewpoints series)
    Includes bibliographical references and index.
    ISBN 0-7377-2228-2 (lib. bdg. : alk. paper) —
    ISBN 0-7377-2229-0 (pbk. : alk. paper)
       1. Public schools—United States. 2. School choice—United States. 3. Multicultural education—United States. 4. Religion in the public schools—United States. I. Title: Opposing viewpoints. II. Williams, Mary E., 1960– .
    LA217.2.E37 2005
    371.01'0973—dc22   2004042454

Printed in the United States of America

"Congress shall make no law...abridging the freedom of speech, or of the press."

First Amendment to the U.S. Constitution

The basic foundation of our democracy is the First Amendment guarantee of freedom of expression. The Opposing Viewpoints Series is dedicated to the concept of this basic freedom and the idea that it is more important to practice it than to enshrine it.

Contents

Why Consider Opposing Viewpoints?

"The only way in which a human being can make some approach to knowing the whole of a subject is by hearing what can be said about it by persons of every variety of opinion and studying all modes in which it can be looked at by every character of mind. No wise man ever acquired his wisdom in any mode but this."

John Stuart Mill

In our media-intensive culture it is not difficult to find differing opinions. Thousands of newspapers and magazines and dozens of radio and television talk shows resound with differing points of view. The difficulty lies in deciding which opinion to agree with and which "experts" seem the most credible. The more inundated we become with differing opinions and claims, the more essential it is to hone critical reading and thinking skills to evaluate these ideas. Opposing Viewpoints books address this problem directly by presenting stimulating debates that can be used to enhance and teach these skills. The varied opinions contained in each book examine many different aspects of a single issue. While examining these conveniently edited opposing views, readers can develop critical thinking skills such as the ability to compare and contrast authors' credibility, facts, argumentation styles, use of persuasive techniques, and other stylistic tools. In short, the Opposing Viewpoints Series is an ideal way to attain the higher-level thinking and reading skills so essential in a culture of diverse and contradictory opinions.

In addition to providing a tool for critical thinking, Opposing Viewpoints books challenge readers to question their own strongly held opinions and assumptions. Most people form their opinions on the basis of upbringing, peer pressure, and personal, cultural, or professional bias. By reading carefully balanced opposing views, readers must directly confront new ideas as well as the opinions of those with whom they disagree. This is not to simplistically argue that everyone who reads opposing views will—or should— change his or her opinion. Instead, the series enhances readers' understanding of their own views by encouraging confrontation with opposing ideas. Careful examination of others' views can lead to the readers' understanding of the logical inconsistencies in their own opinions, perspective on why they hold an opinion, and the consideration of the possibility that their opinion requires further evaluation.

Evaluating Other Opinions

To ensure that this type of examination occurs, Opposing Viewpoints books present all types of opinions. Prominent spokespeople on different sides of each issue as well as well-known professionals from many disciplines challenge the reader. An additional goal of the series is to provide a forum for other, less known, or even unpopular viewpoints. The opinion of an ordinary person who has had to make the decision to cut off life support from a terminally ill relative, for example, may be just as valuable and provide just as much insight as a medical ethicist's professional opinion. The editors have two additional purposes in including these less known views. One, the editors encourage readers to respect others' opinions—even when not enhanced by professional credibility. It is only by reading or listening to and objectively evaluating others' ideas that one can determine whether they are worthy of consideration. Two, the inclusion of such viewpoints encourages the important critical thinking skill of objectively evaluating an author's credentials and bias. This evaluation will illuminate an author's reasons for taking a particular stance on an issue and will aid in readers' evaluation of the author's ideas.

It is our hope that these books will give readers a deeper understanding of the issues debated and an appreciation of the complexity of even seemingly simple issues when good and honest people disagree. This awareness is particularly important in a democratic society such as ours in which people enter into public debate to determine the common good. Those with whom one disagrees should not be regarded as enemies but rather as people whose views deserve careful examination and may shed light on one's own.

Thomas Jefferson once said that "difference of opinion leads to inquiry, and inquiry to truth." Jefferson, a broadly educated man, argued that "if a nation expects to be ignorant and free . . . it expects what never was and never will be." As individuals and as a nation, it is imperative that we consider the opinions of others and examine them with skill and discernment. The Opposing Viewpoints Series is intended to help readers achieve this goal.

David L. Bender and Bruno Leone,
Founders

Greenhaven Press anthologies primarily consist of previously published material taken from a variety of sources, including periodicals, books, scholarly journals, newspapers, government documents, and position papers from private and public organizations. These original sources are often edited for length and to ensure their accessibility for a young adult audience. The anthology editors also change the original titles of these works in order to clearly present the main thesis of each viewpoint and to explicitly indicate the opinion presented in the viewpoint. These alterations are made in consideration of both the reading and comprehension levels of a young adult audience. Every effort is made to ensure that Greenhaven Press accurately reflects the original intent of the authors included in this anthology.

Introduction

"This is education's moment."

—U.S. Department of Education

For several decades, concerns have been raised about the caliber of American education. In 1983, for example, the U.S. Department of Education released a report, *A Nation at Risk*, that proclaimed that the quality of public education had deteriorated since the 1950s. Fifteen years later, a group of educators and policy makers gathered to discuss what had happened with American education since *A Nation at Risk* had been printed. Their conclusions were announced in a 1998 education reform manifesto entitled "A Nation Still at Risk."

According to "A Nation Still at Risk," the quality of U.S. public education in the 1990s remained poor. Since 1983, more than 10 million students had reached their senior year with no basic reading skills, and 20 million had been promoted to the twelfth grade without having learned math fundamentals. During this same period, more than 6 million students dropped out of school.

In response to such dire reports on the state of American education, policy makers have suggested various reforms. Just after President George W. Bush took office in January 2001, for example, he asked Congress to draft bipartisan legislation that would enable all children attending public schools to attain proficiency in essential academic skills. In 2002 Bush signed the resulting No Child Left Behind Act (NCLB) into law. This law amends the 1965 Elementary and Secondary Education Act with reforms focusing on early childhood learning, increased accountability for states, school districts, and schools, enhanced resources, and more local flexibility in the use of federal education funding.

With the passage of NCLB, educators have a mandate to change the culture of America's schools and ensure, by the year 2014, that every American student is academically proficient. Federal funding is targeted to support educational programs and teaching methods that research has revealed to be most effective in improving student achievement. In addition, states must hold all elementary and secondary students to the same challenging academic content and standards. However, states and school districts have flexibility in choosing which specific programs and practices to implement, allowing administrators and teachers to focus on the needs of their particular student populations.

While many educators, parents, and students applaud NCLB's goals of academic proficiency for all students, not everyone agrees with the act's specifications. Among the more controversial features of NCLB are its accountability provisions. Currently, states must define how they address achievement gaps and ensure that all students, including the disadvantaged, attain academic proficiency. They are required to produce annual report cards that inform parents and communities about student and school progress. In doing so, each state must annually measure, through standardized tests, every student's performance in reading and math in grades three through eight and at least once during grades ten through twelve. Schools that fail to make measurable yearly progress toward statewide goals must provide free supplemental services, such as tutoring or after-school assistance; they may also eventually face corrective actions, such as retraining of teachers, staff replacement, and closure and restructuring.

President Bush applauds NCLB's accountability requirements: "Accountability is an exercise in hope. When we raise academic standards, children raise their academic sights. When children are regularly tested, teachers know where and how to improve. When scores are known to parents, parents are empowered to push for change. When accountability for our schools is real, the results for our children are real." But many teachers and policy makers are wary of the law's emphasis on assessment through high-stakes testing. According to Stephanie Fanjul, student achievement director of the National Education Association (NEA), "Every teacher knows tests have a role to play. Teachers use tests all the time, including standardized tests. We want to be sure our students are learning and growing. But there are lots of ways that we collect that information, not just tests. Almost never does a bubble sheet reflect back the breadth of what a child understands. When tests are punitive, all the attention is focused on the scores. That doesn't help educate our children."

Research provides support for Fanjul's concerns. According to a comprehensive study conducted by scientists at Arizona State University, high-stakes testing does not boost student achievement. Researchers examined the results of several well-regarded national tests, including the National Assessment of Education Progress, the SAT, and the ACT. They found that states that had implemented their own high-stakes tests showed no improvement on the national tests. Although scores on the state tests *did* improve over time, scores on the national tests did not. As NEA spokesman Alain Jehlen explains, "Higher [state] test scores were apparently due to the enormous amounts of time and effort that schools poured into teaching the content and exact wording patterns that students would see on these particular tests. The improvement did not carry over into better performance on the other tests of the same general content—they did not reflect real gains in learning."

As the above research findings suggest, high-stakes testing could encourage teachers to teach students how to take specific tests rather than how to apply knowledge. Opponents of NCLB contend that effective preschool programs, smaller class sizes, quality teachers, parental involvement, and up-to-date textbooks and technology would boost student performance far more effectively than high-stakes testing would. It will take years, however, to accurately gauge the effects of NCLB, and it is possible that this federal education law will be amended and altered in the future.

The broad range of concerns and suggestions for education reform reveals that there is no quick solution to the nation's educational problems. *Opposing Viewpoints: Education* examines the state of public schools and explores how education can be improved for current and future generations. The authors debate some of the most discussed issues in education in these chapters: What Is the State of Education? Are Alternatives to Public Education Viable? What Role Should Religious and Moral Values Play in Public Education? How Could Public Education Be Improved? This volume offers readers insight into the complexity of national debates on education and education reform.

CHAPTER 1

What Is the State of Education?

Chapter Preface

In debates about the quality of education in America, analysts often point to scores on well-known standardized tests to determine whether overall student performance has improved over time. In one recent study conducted by the College Board, for example, researchers found that both the verbal and math scores of high school seniors taking the Scholastic Aptitude Test (SAT) had declined between 1987 and 1997—continuing a trend that actually began in the mid-1960s. Between 1987 and 1997, however, average grade point averages had risen—from 3.07 to 3.22. In another study, the creators of the American College Test (ACT) noted that students who received B averages at "high-performing" schools scored 26 on the ACT while students who received the same grades at "low-performing" schools scored an average of 19 on the college entrance exam.

What might account for such discrepancies? Many experts place the blame on "grade inflation"—a rise in the overall grade point average with no corresponding rise in student performance. Critics argue that grade inflation occurs when teachers lower their academic standards, enabling students to earn relatively high grades for average or inferior work. According to some researchers, the problem of grade inflation started at U.S. colleges in the 1960s, when an increasing number of professors held negative attitudes toward grades and were more concerned with pleasing students. Over time, the phenomenon spread to high schools, critics assert, where it causes damage by giving students an unrealistic idea of their abilities. Consequently, many "A" students find that they may need remedial coursework as they enter college, and many college admissions panels no longer see grades as a reliable measure of achievement. As Bradford Wilson, executive director of the National Association of Scholars, states: "Grade inflation deflates those who are robbed of their rightful distinction, and it harms those who could benefit from a confirmation of the need for improvement in the light of excellence."

Researchers, however, disagree on the prevalence of grade inflation and the significance of standardized test scores.

Many national groups representing teachers discount the claim that grades are unusually high. In fact, a study conducted by Rand researchers concluded that math and science grades actually *deflated* during the 1980s and 1990s, when coursework became more demanding. In addition, some observers maintain that claims about declining student performance are exaggerated. They point out that the gradual drop in the average SAT score is not an accurate indicator of student progress because school populations have changed since the 1960s, when most students who took the college entrance exam were wealthy and educationally privileged. "When America democratized higher education by opening up the doors of the universities to millions of middle- and working-class people, to black, brown, poor, and rural people, SAT scores dropped only 5 percent below those of the wealthy elite," argues education professor David C. Berliner. "It's a miracle how well ordinary American youth performed against the . . . privileged classes. . . . [It's] a triumph for public education."

While analysts and educators may agree about the need to improve America's public school system, many dispute the claim that U.S. student performance has generally declined. The authors in the following chapter present differing opinions on the state of public education and on several factors that may hinder its progress.

*"The overall evidence on student
achievement is 'unmistakably grim.'"*

The Quality of Public
Education Has Declined

Tom Bethell

The quality of public education in the United States has deteriorated, argues Tom Bethell in the following viewpoint.
Despite recent reform efforts, national and international test
scores reveal that American student performance has gradually declined since 1970, states Bethell. He maintains that in-
efficient bureaucracies, irresponsible teachers' unions, light-
weight curricula, and a lack of teacher preparedness have
created this ongoing crisis in American education. Bethell is
a media fellow at Stanford University's Hoover Institution, a
public policy research foundation.

As you read, consider the following questions:
1. According to Bethell, how do test scores among U.S.
   minority students today compare with minority scores of
   twenty years ago?
2. According to Williamson M. Evers, why has the math
   curriculum been "watered down"?
3. On average, how much does the U.S. government spend
   per student each year, according to the author?

In February [2003], the Hoover Institution's Koret Task Force on K–12 Education met in Washington [D.C.] to present a progress report on American schools. The symposium was held 20 years after the National Commission on Excellence in Education had severely criticized U.S. education. Its report, *A Nation at Risk*, found that U.S. schools, once the envy of the world, were in sharp decline. "A rising tide of mediocrity," the commission noted in its most quoted sentence, "threatens our very future as a Nation and a people."

After months of investigation, the Hoover Institution's task force of experts has found little or no progress. Some things indeed have changed. A great deal more money is being spent on primary and high school education. The budget of the Department of Education rose from $14 billion to $55 billion. Teachers' salaries have risen. Classroom size has been reduced. But these changes have not translated into improved teaching or student achievement. Performance remains flat.

Educational Disarmament

Addressing the Hoover symposium, Secretary of Education Rod Paige commended the Koret Task Force for its "vigilance" and its "concern for America's children." A 378-page book, *Our Schools and Our Future*, published by the Hoover Institution Press, was released at the time of the symposium. It "provides important insights into the education challenges that face us as a nation," Secretary Paige commented.

Some of the main Koret Task Force findings are as follows: The United States continues to fall behind many other countries. Scholastic Aptitude Test [SAT] scores remain well below their 1970 levels. The school year is about seven days shorter than formerly. The share of teachers with a master's degree in a particular subject area (rather than in education) has fallen from 17 percent in 1982 to 5 percent now. Teachers' salaries rose from $19,000 a year to $35,000 in 2000. And their fringe benefits have increased rapidly.

As its title suggested, *A Nation at Risk* invoked a national security rationale for reversing the deteriorating trend of U.S. education. "If an unfriendly foreign power had attempted to impose on America the mediocre educational performance that exists today, we might well have viewed it as an act of war," the report stated. But we had done it to ourselves, in an act of "unilateral educational disarmament."

A Civil Rights Issue

Twenty years later, a new rationale for improving the system was heard. W. Kurt Hauser, the chairman of Hoover's Board of Overseers, said in his introductory remarks that public education has become a "civil rights issue." Poor black and Hispanic children, who find themselves stuck in inner-city schools where not much is learned, lack the opportunities enjoyed by middle-class children to move to better schools. The solution is to "introduce a competitive environment, accountability and choice," Hauser said. "Let market forces empower parents with alternatives to government monopoly of the schools."

School vouchers could do this. Since 1990, when a public voucher program was enacted in Milwaukee, reformers have sought to provide vouchers to poor and minority families.[1] As Hoover senior fellow Terry Moe pointed out, the argument for vouchers these days has less to do with introducing competition into the system than with social equity. Disadvantaged kids should be given immediate opportunities to get out of bad schools.

This "has put the opponents of vouchers in an extremely awkward position," Moe continued. "As liberals, they claim to be (and usually are) champions of the poor. But on the voucher issue, they refuse to represent their own constituents —and indeed find themselves fighting *against* poor families, who are only trying to escape conditions that liberals agree are deplorable."

In his report on "Minority Children at Risk," Koret Task Force member Paul T. Hill (with coauthors Kacey Guin and Mary Beth Celio) points out that minority students were doing poorly 20 years ago. Their test scores "have increased marginally, if at all, since. The gaps between minority and white achievement are as great now as then."

Their numbers are also increasing. In 1983, Hispanics

---

1. Vouchers enable parents to use state funds to send their children to private schools.

made up 9 percent of K–12 public school students. By 1999, that number had risen to 16 percent. (For blacks, the increase was more modest—from 16 percent to 17 percent.) Minority students are highly concentrated in the inner cities, where for a variety of reasons it is much more difficult to impart knowledge and good learning habits. Today, blacks and Hispanics form an actual majority of students in 46 out of 57 big-city school districts. Although there are 15,000 school districts nationwide, a mere 10 districts educate 19 percent of all black schoolchildren.

"There is reason to fear that simple comparisons of average scores for whites and minorities mask a troubling fact—that one-third or more of minority students in urban schools perform at extremely low levels," Paul Hill writes. The teachers' unions and bureaucracies that exercise so much control over the schools have their greatest influence in the big-city public school systems.

The Union Imperative

The incentives of the teachers' unions provide an analytic key to understanding both the decline of public education and the prospects for reform. The union imperative is to maintain membership, to protect teachers' jobs, and to increase pay and fringe benefits. And the political power of the unions allows them to block "almost everything that they don't want," Terry Moe told the conference. "That's going to be the reality for the foreseeable future." But smaller classroom size increases the demand for teachers, so that reform was allowed.

The main reforms the Hoover Task Force recommends—accountability, transparency, and school choice—will be bitterly opposed by the unions. Accountability highlights the performance of schools and teachers. Bad ones can be fired, good ones rewarded. School choice will allow parents to remove their kids from failing schools. "When kids leave, money flows out of unionized schools," Moe said. "So the unions will have fewer members, fewer resources, and less political power."

As to what has changed in 20 years, and what has not, Paul E. Peterson, the Henry Lee Shattuck Professor of Government at Harvard and a member of the Koret Task Force, notes that we are spending more money on education today, in real terms. Yet what has not changed is "the gap between the haves and the have-nots in our society. There are some pluses, if you look for them, but there are also some very clear minuses." Corrected for inflation, we are spending three times more per child than we spent in 1960.

The overall evidence on student achievement is "unmistakably grim," Peterson said. In reading and writing, there are "multiple signs of a downward trend." At the same time, the percentage of students finishing high school has steadily declined.

The U.S. Compared to Other Nations

How do we compare with other countries? Historically, the American education system has compared favorably with that of other countries. As late as 1970, a higher percentage of young people in America finished high school than did their peers in any other country. By the late 1990s, however, the United States had fallen to about average among the advanced industrial democracies, ranking behind Japan, Korea, Germany, France, Ireland, and other countries.

In the Third International Mathematics and Science Tests, American students ranked closer to the international average (among 38 participating nations) than to that of students in the highest performing countries: Singapore, Korea, Japan, Belgium, Hong Kong, and the Netherlands. American standing in the world deteriorates as students move into higher grades. At the age of 9, American students do reasonably well. But among 17-year-olds, the United States ranks near the bottom of participating countries.

These results are consistent with the National Assessment of Educational Progress [NAEP] tests in math, reading, and science administered to a cross section of all students at ages 9, 13, and 17. NAEP, too, shows that the U.S. education system, somewhat strong at the elementary level, weakens as students move through school.

The mathematics curriculum has been watered down, "in the faint hope that it will be more fun, and exciting for students," Hoover fellow and task force member Williamson M.

Evers said. "Math appreciation," rather than serious mathematics, is making headway.

E.D. Hirsch Jr., an emeritus professor at the University of Virginia and Koret Task Force member, said that one of the problems is that teachers are not expected to impart a coherent curriculum in the early grades. If students are not exposed to a rich diet of knowledge at home, "they never acquire the tools they need to succeed, such as the ability to read with understanding," he said. Reading is not just an abstract skill; it is also dependent on knowledge.

Hirsch located the problem "not so much in the unions as in the intellectual attitudes in the schools of education," which remain dominated by "romantic ideas." The problems in our schools can be corrected "only when our schools of education return to the emphasis on knowledge that once guided our primary schools, and still guide those in the Asian countries that outperform the U.S. by a wide margin."

Spending Does Not Lead to Improvement

Senator Lamar Alexander of Tennessee, who was the secretary of education under former president [George H.W.] Bush, addressed the symposium, along with Milton Goldberg, who was executive director of the commission that produced *A Nation at Risk*. At one point Senator Alexander offered an unfashionable diagnosis of what ails the system. It "contravenes the conventional wisdom," he admitted, that "not enough money" is going to the right places. He allowed that the evidence from the District of Columbia with "lots of money, and poor results" contradicts this. Average spending in the United States is $8,100 per pupil. Hoover Task Force member Herbert J. Walberg recently calculated that the average per-pupil spending in Washington, D.C., is close to $11,000 and that the dropout rate is about 40 percent.

Several members of the Koret Task Force said that there is no evidence that more money yields improvement in the classroom. Performance is unrelated to dollars spent, said Hoover senior fellow Eric A. Hanushek. "Performance has been flat in the United States and yet spending has been going up dramatically for a century." Chester Finn, a walking encyclopedia of all things educational and chairman of the task force, said that more money "hasn't worked, isn't working, and after 20 years how much more experiment with failure do we need?"

An argument sometimes heard is that the great American middle class is more or less content with its (primarily suburban) schools. They rate their own schools B plus, everyone else's C minus. In just the same way, people often think that their own hospital, and their own member of Congress, is good and all the others are bad. (The "retail fallacy," sociologists call it.) So parents are often wary of reforms because they worry that their own schools could lose out to others in a zero-sum reshuffle. Thus middle-class pressure for reform of the system is not intense enough to counteract the unions' resistance.

"Well, the suburban schools are not working as well as people tend to think," Chester Finn said. "The great American middle class is under a bit of an illusion that its schools are just fine. Compare them with student achievement in Germany or Japan or Korea or a wide range of other countries, and we can show that it just isn't true."

Participants generally agreed that unless the system becomes more transparent (so that parents and reformers have better information about what is going on); more accountable (teachers, schools, and school districts can be rewarded for their successes and penalized for their failures); and allows parents to choose the school their kids may attend, the needed improvements will not take place. There was also an undercurrent of sentiment that in the immediate future, and perhaps for some time to come, the teachers' unions will have enough political clout to block needed reforms. If so, and particularly if school choice is stymied, the gap between the suburban schools and those in the inner cities will continue to widen.

Eventually, it will become plain for all to see that government education is one civil right that the usual defenders of civil rights are not very interested in. At the moment, the problem can be put this way: A continued political alliance with the teachers' unions is more valuable to the advocates of civil rights than is the literacy and education of minorities. On the day that complacency on this issue dissolves, the enemies of reform will be in trouble.

"We should think more than twice before we tinker too much with an educational system that encourages questioning."

The Quality of Public Education Has Not Declined

Gerald W. Bracey

In the viewpoint that follows, Gerald W. Bracey contends that there is no great crisis in American education. As Bracey points out, critics of public education often compare U.S. students' test scores to those of their international counterparts and claim that American students are falling behind. These critics, however, fail to acknowledge that the United States ranks high in competitiveness, granting it an economic edge in the global arena. In Bracey's view, American competitiveness, innovation, and creativity are not linked to test scores but to a generally good educational system that encourages questioning and critical thinking. Bracey is an educational researcher and writer in Alexandria, Virginia.

As you read, consider the following questions:
1. What rank does the United States have on the World Economic Forum's Current Competitiveness Index, according to Bracey?
2. In the author's opinion, what might discourage innovative thinking?
3. What happened when author Amy Biancolli tried to get her Scottish students to discuss Shakespeare, according to Bracey?

Gerald W. Bracey, "What Crisis?" *Washington Post National Weekly Edition*, vol. 19, May 13–19, 2002, p. 23. Copyright © 2002 by Gerald W. Bracey. Reproduced by permission.

There's no pleasing some people, even when they get what they want. So why do we keep listening to them? For almost 20 years now, some of our most prominent business leaders and politicians have sounded the same alarm about the nation's public schools. It began in earnest with that 1983 golden treasury of selected, spun and distorted education statistics, *A Nation At Risk*, whose authors wrote, "If only to keep and improve on the slim competitive edge we retain in world markets, we must dedicate ourselves to the reform of our educational system. . . ."

The document tightly yoked our economic position in the world to how well or poorly students bubbled in answer sheets on standardized tests.

And it continued in September 2000, when a national commission on math and science teaching headed by former Ohio senator John Glenn issued a report titled "Before It's Too Late." It asked, rhetorically, "In an integrated, global economy . . . will our children be able to compete?"

The report's entirely predictable answer: Not if we don't improve schools *"before it's too late"* (emphasis in the original report).

So you might think that these Chicken Littles would be firing up their fax machines and e-mailing everywhere to report the following hot news from the World Economic Forum's "Global Competitiveness Report, 2001–2002": The United States ranks second in the organization's Current Competitiveness Index (CCI), trailing only Finland.

The CCI isn't just another survey. It is a sophisticated rating system derived from a wide variety of economic and other factors, including education data. And the World Economic Forum (or WEF) isn't some minor league player. Its annual conference draws a cross-section of the planet's most powerful political and business leaders—including some of the people so concerned about America's schools.

But the naysayers haven't trumpeted the CCI ranking. Indeed, I wouldn't be surprised if, sometime soon, a leading member of Congress or the business community declares that we must reform our educational system to maintain our competitive edge—or best those pesky Finns.

'Twas ever thus. Schools often take the hit for bad turns

of events, but somehow never get the credit for upturns. Remember 1957? The Russians launched Sputnik, the first manmade satellite to orbit Earth. When people asked how we could lose the race to space, public schools were an easy target. *Life* magazine ran a five-part series on the "Crisis in Education." Major universities assumed the role of rescuers to develop modern, challenging textbooks. In 1969, America put a man on the moon, a destination that the Russians—with their allegedly superior scientists—never reached. Did a magazine declare an end to the "crisis" in education? Do pigs fly?

I don't mean to suggest, of course, that America's public schools are perfect. The dreary state of some urban and poor rural school systems is well documented. But I've been following the angst over our competitive capabilities since the 1983 report, and I've noticed the same pattern. In the early 1990s, as the economy tanked and a recession set in, many variations of "lousy-schools-are-producing-a-lousy-work-force-and-it's-killing-us-in-the-global-marketplace" could be heard. But these slackers somehow managed to turn things around: By early 1994, many publications featured banner headlines about the recovery that later became the longest sustained period of growth in the nation's history. "The American Economy: Back on Top" was the way that the *New York Times* summed up the turnabout in Feb. 1994.

Well, if the schools took the rap when the economy went south, surely they would be praised when the economy boomed, right? Hardly. A mere three months after the *Times* story appeared, IBM CEO Louis V. Gerstner Jr., wrote an op-ed for for the *Times* headlined "Our Schools Are Failing."

They are failing, said Gerstner, because they are not producing students who can compete with their international peers.

Success Is Not Linked to Test Scores

The bashers have kept up their drumbeat. Intel CEO Craig R. Barrett, Texas Instruments CEO Thomas Engibous, State Farm Insurance CEO Edward Rust and then-Wisconsin Gov. Tommy Thompson all took to the nations op-ed pages in 2000 and 2001 to lament the threat that our education system poses to our competitiveness. Gerstner made an encore appearance on the *Times* op-ed page in March [2002], expressing his continuing concern that our schools will "limit our competitive position in the global marketplace."

American Education Is Improving

The Koret Task Force does a valuable service for American education. Its recommendations are largely on target as we stick with the task of improving our schools and move toward the goal of "leaving no child behind." But I see the events of the past 20 years in a different light. Our educators, students, parents, and policymakers deserve much more credit for what has been accomplished. While improvement has come in fits and starts—and detoured into a number of dead-ends—American education is better today than it was in 1983. And we are on the verge of making it much better.

James B. Hunt Jr., *Education Next*, Spring 2003.

None of these fine gentlemen provided any data on the relationship between the economy's health and the performance of schools. Our long economic boom suggests there isn't one—or that our schools are better than the critics claim. But there is a broader, more objective means of looking for any relationship. The Third International Mathematics and Science Study (TIMSS) provides test scores for 41 nations, including the United States. Thirty-eight of those countries are ranked on the World Economic Forum's CCI. It's a simple statistical matter to correlate the test scores with the CCI.

There is little correlation. The United States is 29th in mathematics, but second in competitiveness. Korea is third in mathematics, but 27th in competitiveness. And so forth. If the two lists had matched, place for place, that would produce a perfect correlation of +1.0. But because some countries are high on competitiveness and low on test scores (and vice versa), the actual correlation is +.23. In the world of statistics, this is considered quite small.

Actually, even that small correlation is misleadingly high: Seven countries are low on both variables, creating what little relationship there is. If these seven nations are removed from the calculation, the correlation between test scores and competitiveness actually becomes negative, meaning that higher test scores are slightly associated with lower competitiveness.

The education variables in the index include: the quality of schools; the TIMSS scores; the number of years of education and the proportion of the country's population attending college (these two are variables in which the United States excels); and survey rankings from executives who, the World Economic Forum claims, have "international perspectives." The WEF ranked U.S. schools 27th of the 75 nations—not exactly eye-popping, but given all of the horrible things said about American schools in the past 25 years, perhaps surprisingly high. (The United States looked particularly bad in one WEF category: the difference in quality between rich and poor schools. We finished 42nd, lower than any other developed nation. That is shameful in a country as rich as ours.)

The Importance of Innovative Thinking

So, if 26 nations have better schools, how did we earn our No. 2 overall competitiveness ranking? The WEF uses dozens of variables from many sectors, and the United States rates well across the board.

One important consideration is the "brain drain" factor. Our scientists and engineers stay here, earning us a top ranking in this category. No other country, not even Finland, came close on this measurement.

But what really caught my eye were the top U.S. scores on a set of variables that make up what the WEF calls "National Innovation Capacity." Innovation variables are critical to competitiveness, according to the WEF. Ten years ago, the competitive edge was gained by nations that could lower costs and raise quality. Virtually all developed countries have accomplished this, the WEF report asserts, and thus "competitive advantage must come from the ability to create and then commercialize new products and processes, shifting the technology frontier as fast as rivals can catch up."

Innovation is itself a complicated affair, but my guess is that it is not linked to test scores. If anything, too much testing discourages innovative thinking.

American schools, believe it or not, have developed a culture that encourages innovative thinking. How many other cultures do that? A 2001 op-ed in the *Washington Post* was titled "At Least Our Kids Ask Questions."

In the essay, author Amy Biancolli described her travails in trying to get Scottish students to discuss Shakespeare. She found that they weren't used to being allowed to express their opinions or having them valued. I had the same experience when I taught college students in Hong Kong. Years later, I mentioned this to a professor in Taiwan who said that even today, "professors' questions are often met with stony silence."

An Edge in Creativity

We take our questioning culture so much for granted that we don't even notice it until we encounter another country that doesn't have it. A 2001 *New York Times* article discussed, in the words of Japanese scientists, why Americans win so many Nobel prizes while the Japanese win so few.

The Japanese scientists provided a number of reasons, but the one they cited as most important was peer review. Before American scientists publish their research, they submit it to the scrutiny—questioning—of other researchers. Japanese culture discourages this kind of direct confrontation; one Japanese scientist recalled his days in the United States, when he would watch scholars—good friends—engage in furious battles, challenging and testing each other's assumptions and logic. That would never happen in Japan, he told the *Times* reporter.

Japan's culture of cooperation and consensus makes for a more civil society than we find here, but our combative culture leaves as with an edge in creativity.

We should think more than twice before we tinker too much with an educational system that encourages questioning. We won't benefit from one that idolizes high test scores.

It could put our very competitiveness as a nation at risk.

"*[Universities offer] a smorgasbord of attacks on Western civilization that are a part of the so-called multicultural agenda.*"

An Emphasis on Diversity Has Harmed Education

Roger Kimball

A focus on diversity and multiculturalism at U.S. colleges and universities is undermining higher education, contends Roger Kimball in the following viewpoint. Campuses that claim to nurture diversity have largely left-wing faculties who persuade students to adopt liberal opinions on controversial issues, Kimball maintains. He argues that this lack of genuine political diversity at colleges has resulted in a biased curriculum that denigrates Western civilization and discourages intellectual rigor. Kimball is managing editor of the *New Criterion* and author of *Tenured Radicals*.

As you read, consider the following questions:

1. What kinds of incidents prove the predominance of left-wing opinion on college campuses, according to Kimball?
2. According to a study cited by the author, how many history professors at Brown University are liberal? How many are conservative?
3. According to a 2001 Frank Luntz poll, what percentage of Ivy League professors is Republican?

Roger Kimball, "Academia vs. America," *American Legion*, vol. 154, April 2003, pp. 35–38. Copyright © 2003 by Roger Kimball. Reproduced by permission.

In the 1960s and 1970s, the famous commentator Susan Sontag made a career of promoting highbrow anti-Americanism. America, she complained was a "mechanized, anxious, television-brainwashed" society, a country "founded on genocide" and that in its maturity indulged in a "lethal" barbarism. She described America as cancerous, inorganic, dead, coercive and authoritarian. After the World Trade Center was destroyed on Sept. 11, 2001, she wrote in the *New Yorker* magazine: "Where is the acknowledgment that this was not a 'cowardly' attack on 'civilization' or 'liberty' or 'humanity' or 'the free world' but an attack on the world's self-proclaimed superpower, undertaken as a consequence of specific American alliances and actions?"

While most Americans expressed outrage about the attacks, the prevailing elite liberal opinion was more likely to search for an excuse, an extenuation, a rationalization, anything but a clear-cut denunciation for an unwarranted act of terrorism. Immediately after the attacks, Reuters news agency refused to describe the perpetrators as terrorists. The reasoning was that one man's terrorist was another man's freedom fighter. Not everyone went as far as the playwright Harold Pinter, who described the United States as "the greatest source of terrorism on earth." But many liberal commentators agreed with the classicist Mary Beard, who reported that in England many people felt that "however tactfully you dress it up, the United States had it coming."

Academia's Anti-Americanism

Nowhere are such sentiments more common than in academia. Consider the case of Barbara Foley, a professor of English at Rutgers University in New Jersey. In the wake of the deadly assaults on New York and Washington, Foley posted a message on the Internet for her students. It dealt partly with readings for the class, partly with the terrorist attacks. "We should be aware that, whatever its proximate cause," Foley wrote, "its ultimate cause is the fascism of u.s. [sic] foreign policy over the past many decades."

Take the much-publicized case of Peter N. Kirstein, a tenured professor of history at St. Xavier University in Chicago. [In the fall of 2002], Kirstein received a form e-mail letter from a cadet at the U.S. Air Force Academy soliciting help publicizing a symposium on the theme "America's Challenges in an Unstable World: Balancing Security with Liberty." Kirstein's response deserves to be quoted verbatim:

> You are a disgrace to this country and I am furious you would even think I would support you and your aggressive baby killing tactics of collateral damage. Help you recruit. Who, top guns to reign [sic] death and destruction upon nonwhite peoples throughout the world? Are you serious sir? Resign your commission and serve your country with honour. No war, no air force cowards who bomb countries without AAA, without possibility of retaliation. You are worse than the snipers. You are imperialists who are turning the whole damn world against us. September 11 can be blamed in part for what you and your cohorts have done to the Palestinians, the VC, the Serbs, a retreating army at Basra. You are unworthy of my support.

Takes your breath away, doesn't it? St. Xavier reprimanded Kirstein and relieved him of his teaching duties for a semester. Under pressure, he apologized for the message but presumably will soon be back molding young minds.

Selective Diversity

The great irony lurking behind these examples, which could easily be multiplied, centers on the word "diversity." What quality above all others do college administrators and teachers strive to nurture on campus these days? Intellectual rigor? Not likely. After all, rigor presupposes maintaining high standards, and, as we hear repeatedly, high standards are invidious. Houston Baker, a former president of the Modern Language Association, spoke for some in his profession when he said that choosing between Shakespeare and Jacqueline Susann, for instance, is "no different from choosing between a hoagy and a pizza."

"I am one whose career is dedicated to the day when we have a disappearance of those standards," Baker said.

Ironically, "diversity" means "variety," yet campuses across America actually encourage strict conformity on all contentious issues. We have read the stories: the case of campus A, which champions diversity but looks the other way when a conservative student newspaper is confiscated and destroyed; or campus B, where the women's studies program refuses to welcome women who are pro-life; or campus C, where administrators and many prominent faculty members mounted a campaign to prevent the establishment of a local chapter of the National Association of Scholars, a traditional-minded group of teachers whose motto is "For Reasoned Scholarship in a Free Society."

Consider this item from the University of California–Berkeley English department's fall 2002 course catalog. It was for English R1A, "The Politics and Poetics of Palestinian Resistance," which would earn students four units toward a degree:

> The brutal Israeli military occupation of Palestine, [ongoing] since 1948, has systematically displaced, killed and maimed millions of Palestinian people. And yet, from under the brutal weight of the occupation, Palestinians have produced their own culture and poetry of resistance. This class will examine the history of the [resistance] and the way that it is narrated by Palestinians in order to produce an understanding of the Intifada. . . . This class takes as its starting point the right of Palestinians to fight for their own self-determination. Conservative thinkers are encouraged to seek other sections.

"The Politics and Poetics of Palestinian Resistance" is not an academic or scholarly inquiry. It will not attempt to step back and assess the merits of arguments for and against a certain interpretation of historical events. On the contrary, "conservative thinkers are encouraged to seek other sections." After news of this class made national headlines, Berkeley administrators removed that line, but the class went forward.

Left-Wing Faculty

The accumulation of anecdotal evidence tells us a lot, but hard data also exists to convince skeptics. *American Enterprise* magazine provided a revealing picture of the political diversity of college faculties in "The Shame of America's One-Party Campuses," an article from its September 2002 issue. "Today's colleges and universities," the article notes, "are *not*, to use the current buzzword, 'diverse' places. Quite the opposite: they are virtual one-party states, ideological monopolies, badly unbalanced ecosystems. . . . They do not, when it comes to political and cultural ideas, look like America."

To support this claim, *American Enterprise*—with some help from the California-based Center for the Study of Popular Culture—visited local boards of elections in the neighborhoods of more than 20 major colleges and universities. They then cross-referenced voter-registration records with faculty rosters for several major departments.

The results were hardly surprising.

At Brown University, for example, five professors of economics were registered in a party of the left, but only one on the right. In engineering, seven were on the left, two on the right.

In the English department, 10 were on the left and none were on the right.

What about history? Seventeen on the left, zero on the right.

Political science? Seven to zero.

Sociology? Eight to zero.

Diversity Dishonesty on College Campuses

Diversity, multiculturalism, tolerance, and political correctness are the watchwords in colleges and universities today. The campus thought police have defined those words to enforce the liberal leftwing agenda. Diversity means diversity only for thoughts and practices that are politically correct. Political correctness means conformity to leftwing orthodoxy. Multiculturalism means all cultures are equal but Western Judeo-Christian civilization is the worst. Tolerance means acceptance of all behaviors except those that comport with the Ten Commandments.

Phyllis Schlafly, *Phyllis Schlafly Report*, April 2002.

Brown is not an anomaly. At the State University of New York, 15 faculty members in sociology were registered in a party of the left and zero on the right. In political science, the ratio is 20 to 1. At the University of Colorado-Boulder; it's 37 to 0 in English; 28 to 1 in history; 14 to 0 in journalism and 17 to 2 in political science.

The pattern is the same at Harvard, Davidson College, Penn State University, UC-Berkeley, Syracuse University, Pomona College and the University of Maryland. Ditto at

Stanford, UCLA and the University of California at Santa Barbara. Among more than 200 faculty members at Williams College, only four are registered Republicans.

The *American Enterprise* survey also reports on a poll of 151 Ivy League professors. Conducted by Frank Luntz Research in 2001, the poll found 3 percent of those surveyed identified themselves as Republican (none identified themselves as "conservative"; 6 percent checked "somewhat conservative"). As for voting, the Luntz survey reported that 84 percent of Ivy League professors voted for Al Gore, 9 percent for George W. Bush and 6 percent for Ralph Nader. The U.S. electorate at large was divided between the major candidates, with 48 percent each for Gore and Bush.

Havens for Displaced Radicals

What do these surveys tell us? For one thing, as *American Enterprise* notes, they tell us that although "colleges like to characterize themselves as wide-open places . . . where all ideals and principles may be pursued freely," in reality "you will find a much wider—and freer—cross-section of human reasoning and conviction in the aisles of any grocery store or city bus."

The wildly skewed political complexion of college faculties is grounds for concern. Among other things, it shows what a travesty the touted ideal of diversity is on many campuses. But more is at stake than a spurious ideal of diversity. In a deeper sense, we are facing not a mere failure but an active repudiation of education as traditionally conceived.

Universities used to be dedicated to the advancement of knowledge. It was understood that if they were to be successful, they had to presuppose what the 19th-century British poet and critic Matthew Arnold called the ideal of "disinterestedness." In describing criticism as "disinterested," Arnold did not mean that it speaks without reference to a particular point of view. Rather, he meant a habit of inquiry that refused to lend itself to any "ulterior, political, practical considerations about ideas." We might say that Arnold looked to criticism to provide a bulwark against ideology, something that John Searle, a different sort of Berkeley professor, said with his customary lucidity in his 1990 essay "The Storm Over the University": "The idea that the curriculum should be converted to any partisan purposes is a perversion of the ideal of the university."

Since the 1960s, however, universities have become havens for displaced radicals and the humanities' instruments of political agitation. Arnold's vision of the civilizing potential of "the best that has been thought and said" gives way to a smorgasbord of attacks on Western civilization that are a part of the so-called multicultural agenda.

The Fate of Academic Life

It may be tempting to dismiss such examples as nothing more than the twittering of academics—a group, after all, that is notorious for being out of touch with reality. The problem is that the fate of academic life is not only an academic issue. It is an issue that touches deeply on one of the chief crucibles of the future.

In the late 1800s, the German aphorist G.C. Lichtenberg said, "Nowadays we everywhere seek to propagate wisdom: who knows whether in a couple of centuries there may not exist universities for restoring the old ignorance?"

Now we know.

"When students [listen] to different perspectives, they may come to appreciate how such discussions may increase their understanding of an issue."

An Emphasis on Diversity Benefits Education

Patricia G. Avery

Students benefit from a classroom environment that encourages the study and discussion of diverse viewpoints, argues Patricia G. Avery in the following viewpoint. Although college classrooms are known for exposing students to differing opinions, even students at the high school level learn the importance of tolerance when they seriously examine minority views and the role of political dissent in a democracy. Since tolerance is so essential to democracy, Avery writes, U.S. teachers should challenge their students through educational discussions about civil liberties, political dissent, and other controversial issues. Avery is a professor at the University of Minnesota's Department of Curriculum and Instruction in Minneapolis.

As you read, consider the following questions:
1. What kinds of people tend to be more intolerant, according to Avery?
2. In the author's opinion, why do many high-school teachers shy away from classroom discussions of controversial issues?
3. In Avery's view, when is the best time to teach students about tolerance for diversity of belief?

Patricia G. Avery, "Teaching Tolerance: What Research Tells Us," *Social Education*, vol. 66, September 2002, pp. 270–72, 274. Copyright © 2002 by the National Council for the Social Studies. Reproduced by permission.

They first came for the Communists and I didn't speak up because I wasn't a Communist.

Then they came for the Socialists and the Trade Unionists, but I was neither, so I did not speak out.

Then they came for the Jews, but I was not a Jew so I did not speak out.

And when they came for me, there was no one left to speak out for me.

Attributed to Pastor Martin Niemoeller,
a German opponent of Nazism

When U.S. citizens are asked what America means to them, they are most likely to talk about freedoms, liberties, and individual rights. In one study in answer to the question what it means to be American, the typical response was, "Being an American is to be free, to speak up for yourself, to fight for your freedom." Regardless of age, gender, or ethnicity, U.S. citizens tend to associate their country with individual freedoms and rights, particularly freedom of speech, freedom of religion, the right to assemble, and the right to a trial by a jury of peers. Yet in the aftermath of the tragedy of September 11, 2001, polls indicate that many U.S. citizens are willing to accept restrictions on their freedoms in exchange for greater security. One month after the terrorist attack, 42 percent of those polled did not feel it was "okay" to criticize President George W. Bush on domestic or economic issues.

Clearly, no rights are absolute. In 1919, Justice Oliver Wendell Holmes said, "The most stringent protection of free speech would not protect a man in falsely shouting fire in a theatre and causing panic." But the abnegation of civil liberties in a democracy is a very serious proposition and deserves no less than our full attention. The internment of Japanese Americans in the 1940s and the McCarthy hearings in the 1950s are just two of the periods in recent history during which limitations were placed on civil liberties. Today, many U.S. citizens view these events with regret, and believe that the government exceeded its authority.

Political tolerance is the willingness to extend civil liberties to those whose views you find objectionable. You do not demonstrate "tolerance" toward groups whose ideas you support or about which you don't care. For example, if you are sympathetic to the views of a pro-life group, or are neutral toward their stance, then you should not describe yourself as "tolerant" toward the group. It is when you find a group's views quite objectionable that you can truly demonstrate tolerance toward the group.

Each of us has groups whose views ignite our passionate opposition: some examples at different ends of the political spectrum are the Aryan Nation, the National Rifle Association (NRA), the American Civil Liberties Union (ACLU), and People for the Ethical Treatment of Animals (PETA). Pro-life and pro-choice groups are among those that frequently impinge upon core beliefs. It is not easy to grant groups forums for expressing their views when these ideas are in direct opposition to your own.

For more than fifty years, political scientists and psychologists have examined levels of political tolerance among adults and adolescents. In general, the role of demographic characteristics such as age, gender, and socioeconomic status in predicting levels of tolerance is minimal at best. Psychological characteristics, such as level of dogmatism, authoritarianism, and self-esteem are much better predictors of tolerance. Individuals who demonstrate high levels of dogmatism and authoritarianism and low levels of self-esteem are likely to be more intolerant than are their counterparts.

The College Experience

College education is one of the most powerful predictors of tolerance. College experiences seem to decrease authoritarianism and dogmatism, and increase self-esteem, thereby increasing levels of tolerance. It is thought that the college environment exposes students to diverse points of view, either through course readings or interaction with people who hold views in opposition to their own. Even in colleges with a relatively homogeneous student population, young adults learn that it is sometimes helpful to consider alternative perspectives (if only to reflect deeper on one's own position), and that opposing viewpoints need not be threatening.

Secondary school experiences are far less likely to have an impact on students' level of political tolerance than are col-

Developing Thoughtful Citizens

School leaders should recognize that the goals of multicultural education are highly consistent with those of the nation's schools: to develop thoughtful citizens who can function effectively in the world of work and in the civic community. Ways must be found for schools to recognize and respect the cultures and languages of students from diverse groups while at the same time working to develop an overarching national culture to which all groups will have allegiance.

James A. Banks, *School Administrator*, May 1999.

lege experiences. In their interviews with four hundred high school students from four communities throughout the country, [researchers] Conover and Searing found that fewer than 20 percent of the students viewed tolerance as a citizen's duty. One-quarter of the students saw no relationship between tolerance and U.S. citizenship. What accounts for the positive impact of college experiences on students' level of tolerance, and the substantially diminished impact of secondary school experiences? Of course, college students are older and generally more mature. Simply by virtue of their being in college, they also probably represent a more sophisticated and capable group and are more likely than are their secondary school counterparts to be cognitively capable of understanding complex democratic principles, and of seeing the connection between abstract principles and concrete situations. This accounts for some of the difference in the effects of secondary and college experiences on students' level of political tolerance. But, as we shall see, there is more to the story. Curriculum and classroom climate at the secondary level also play an important role in shaping students' level of political tolerance.

Fostering Tolerance

Researchers note that, in general, secondary and college classrooms are very different environments. While the college classroom is expected to be a forum for diverse viewpoints, the secondary classroom is too vulnerable to public pressure to render a serious examination of the role of dissent and dissenters in a democracy. Political scientist Paul Vogt notes that "[precollegiate] educators are unlikely to enhance their careers by courting controversy and discussing the rights of unpopular minorities, to say nothing of advocating those rights." In addition, the pressure for content coverage, the focus on the "basics," and the use of standardized tests all mitigate against secondary teachers examining divergent viewpoints and their role in a democracy.

Traditional secondary texts and classroom practices are also unlikely to foster tolerance because they tend to avoid controversy, but research suggests that curricula specifically designed to teach young people about the role of tolerance in a democracy can have an impact on levels of tolerance. An early study by [D.] Goldenson examined the effects of a three-week civil liberties unit on high school students' level of tolerance. As part of the unit, students conducted in-depth investigations of how the abstract "slogans of democracy" are applied in concrete situations. Students interviewed community members such as police, court officials, and staff at the local American Civil Liberties Union to gain a sense of the complexity of civil liberties issues, as well as the range of perspectives on such issues. Students who took part in the unit demonstrated greater levels of tolerance at the end of the unit, when they were compared to a control group. Goldenson also found that students' perception of the teacher's credibility affected the degree to which tolerance scores improved as a result of the unit. Students who saw their teacher as more credible (e.g., fair, knowledgeable) showed greater increases than did those who perceived the teacher as less credible. . . .

An Open Classroom Climate

There is some evidence to suggest that students' level of political tolerance is related to their perception of the classroom and school environment. First, teachers who actively create an "open classroom climate" demonstrate that they value divergent viewpoints. Second, when students practice listening to different perspectives, they may come to appreciate how such discussions may increase their understanding of an issue. Finally, when students regularly engage in discussions about controversial issues, they are less likely to feel threatened by views that are opposed to their own.

Goldenson's study, previously mentioned, indicated that a curriculum designed to increase students' level of political tolerance had the greatest impact on students who saw their teacher as credible. In the first IEA [International Association for the Evaluation of Educational Achievement] study conducted in 1971, researchers found that student perceptions of teacher encouragement to express their own opinions was positively related to their support for democratic values. [A] secondary analysis of the first IEA civic education data for the United States and West Germany indicated that the best predictors for tolerance of dissent were reports by students that their instruction emphasized causes or explanations of events as opposed to memorizing names or dates, and students' reports that they often talked about current events in class. In the most recent IEA study, the only four countries whose students' attitudes toward women's and immigrants' rights were significantly above the international mean were also among those countries whose students reported a more open classroom climate. [C.L.] Hahn's five-nation study, however, suggested that the relationship between political tolerance and an open classroom climate was insignificant. I suspect that the explanation lies in the interaction between an open classroom climate and a curriculum specifically devoted to civil liberties issues. That is, neither an open classroom climate nor a civil liberties curriculum alone increases students' level of political tolerance, but the combination of the two is likely to promote tolerance. That hypothesis, however, remains to be tested.

Making Sense of Complex Issues

Some may argue that adolescents are too young and too self-absorbed to engage in a sophisticated discussion of civil liberties issues. To be sure, such discussions require a great deal of skill on the part of teachers. But I suggest that adolescence is an ideal time for grappling with civil liberties issues. Young people are beginning to test their rights and consider their responsibilities, they have the ability to link abstract principles ("freedom of speech") with concrete situations, and they are concerned with "in-groups" and "out-groups." In a classroom climate that is supportive of their efforts to make sense of complex public issues, these students can, with practice, come to understand how tolerance is one of the central tenets of a democracy.

It is unclear whether the majority of U.S. citizens will support or protest any government curtailment of civil liberties in the wake of September 11, 2001. But it is hoped that the citizenry will understand the import of their sentiments. Unfortunately, the time to teach about tolerance for diversity of belief is not when citizens feel their security is threatened; rather, it is in times that afford thoughtful deliberation. Those students who develop an appreciation of tolerance and minority rights in quieter times are more likely to recognize the gravity of limiting civil liberties in times of crisis.

"The issue is not highly qualified teachers. The problem is getting teachers who are even decently competent."

Incompetent Teachers Harm Public Education

Thomas Sowell

In the following viewpoint Thomas Sowell contends that American public education faces a crisis because of the low quality of its teachers. In many states, he points out, people can become certified teachers even if they have below average test scores and make low grades in college. Moreover, explains Sowell, training courses for future teachers are so burdensome and substandard that they fail to draw the best students. As a result, highly qualified, intelligent people tend to avoid the field of public school teaching. Sowell is a nationally syndicated columnist.

As you read, consider the following questions:
1. What is the biggest obstacle to getting qualified people teaching in public schools, according to Sowell?
2. In Sowell's opinion, why are alternative routes to teacher certification inadequate?
3. What fact proves that teacher shortages in public schools are not due to low pay, according to the author?

Thomas Sowell, "Teachers Are Why Johnny Can't Read," *Conservative Chronicle*, vol. 17, July 17, 2002, p. 21. Copyright © 2002 by Creators Syndicate, Inc. Reproduced by permission of the author and Creators Syndicate, Inc.

M ost discussions of the problems of American education have an air of utter unreality because they avoid addressing the most fundamental and intractable problem of our public schools—the low quality of our teachers. There is no point expecting teachers to teach things that they themselves do not know or understand.

That becomes painfully obvious from a recently released report from the U.S. Department of Education. This report has an innocuous title on the cover—"Meeting the Highly Qualified Teachers Challenge"—and devastating facts inside.

According to this report, in 28 of the 29 states that use the same standardized test for teachers, it is not even necessary to come up to the national average in mathematics to become a teacher. In none of these states is it necessary to come up to the national average in reading. In some states, you can score in the bottom quarter in either math or reading (or both) and still meet the requirements to become a teacher.

Low Standards for Teaching

This report is only the latest in a long series of studies of teachers, going back more than half a century, showing again and again the low standards for teaching. Those who go into teaching have consistently had test scores at or near the bottom among college students in a wide variety of fields.

Despite the title of this report, the issue is not highly qualified teachers. The problem is getting teachers who are even decently competent. It is a farce and a fraud when teachers' unions talk about a need for "certified" teachers, when certification has such low requirements and when uncertified teachers often have higher qualifications.

Secretary of Education Rod Paige put his finger on the crucial problem when he said that, in selecting teachers, states "maintain low standards and high barriers at the same time." You don't have to know much, but you do have to jump through all kinds of hoops in order to become certified to teach in the public schools.

Education Courses Are Bad

The biggest obstacle are the education courses which can take up years of your time and thousands of dollars of your money, but which have no demonstrated benefit on future teaching. Research shows that teachers' actual knowledge of the subject matter is what benefits students.

Emphasis on something that does not affect educational quality reflects the priorities of the teachers' union in restricting competition, not the requirements for educating children. It would be hard for anyone who has not looked into education courses to believe just how bad they are. I wouldn't believe it myself if I hadn't seen the data, the professors and the students.

Dumbed-Down Teachers

Poor student performance and poor teacher preparation are directly related. In a recent study for the Mackinac Center for Public Policy, Professor Thomas Bertonneau argued that general undergraduate instruction in the state universities is deficient and deteriorating. Far too many graduates lack basic verbal and cognitive abilities, and the reasons are disturbing: the disintegration of an effective core curriculum; the pervasiveness of trendy, politically correct courses that stress indoctrination over genuine learning; the dumbing down of instruction in proper writing and reasoning skills; and a growing gap between what students are taught and what they must know to succeed as teachers or other professionals.

Analyst David P. Doyle describes teacher education in these terms: "It is a classic example of a 'closed' system, one in which there is little or no feedback from the outside world. Once through the process, teachers heave a sigh of relief and get on with their work. Teacher educators, institutionally insulated, have been under little pressure to change or improve. Worse yet, their inertia is reinforced by state teacher licensing requirements that mirror the vapid courses they offer."

Lawrence W. Reed, *Freeman*, January 1997.

People go to these institutions in order to get certified, not because they expect to find anything either interesting or useful. Education courses repel many intelligent people, who are just the sort of people needed in our schools. As Secretary of Education Rod Paige puts it, "schools of education fail to attract the best students." That is an understatement. They repel the best.

Although many states provide alternative routes to teacher

certification, these alternative routes are usually made burdensome enough to protect existing schools of education from losing their students. Indeed, these alternative routes often include many hours of education courses. The net result is that only 6 percent of certified teachers received their certificate via alternative routes. Many such programs, according to the report, "are 'alternative routes' in name only, allowing states to boast of reform while maintaining artificial restrictions on the supply of new teachers."

These artificially created shortages are then used by teachers' unions to argue for higher pay. Secretary Paige does not buy the teachers' union argument that teacher shortages are due to inadequate pay. He points out that "compensation in most private schools is lower than in public schools."

Yet private schools are able to get better qualified people, partly because most private schools do not let education course requirements screen out intelligent people. Some private schools even refuse to hire people who have been through that drivel.

It is refreshing to see a Secretary of Education who says what is wrong in plain English, instead of being a mouthpiece for the status quo in general and the teachers' unions in particular.

> "*Schools do not exist in a vacuum. They are not isolated from their neighborhoods and communities. Inequality in schooling reflects inequality in society.*"

Racial and Economic Inequities Harm Public Education

Duane Campbell

In the viewpoint that follows, Duane Campbell argues that the crisis in American education exists largely in poor urban areas populated by people of color. City schools attended by minorities and the poor are often in disrepair and have insufficient funding, unprepared teachers, scarce educational supplies, and unchallenging curricula. Poor and minority youth must obtain their fair share of educational resources if public schools intend to benefit all students, Campbell asserts. Citizens must choose to increase funding to schools in low-income areas so that youths can receive genuine opportunities, he concludes. Campbell, author of *Choosing Democracy: A Practical Guide to Multicultural Education*, teaches at California State University in Sacramento.

As you read, consider the following questions:

1. What percentage of African American children lives below the poverty line, according to Campbell?
2. According to the author, what have most states done in response to the crisis in urban schools?
3. How much money needs to be spent to improve low-income schools, in Campbell's opinion?

Duane Campbell, "Racism and the Crisis of Urban Education," *Democratic Left*, vol. 30, Winter 2002, pp. 6, 9, 14. Copyright © 2002 by *Democratic Left*.

Quality schools are an issue of human rights for young people. Our public schools should provide all students with a quality education. At present, in urban and poverty areas, they do not. Public schooling is in crisis, particularly for children living in poverty in urban areas. Inequality and white supremacy are created and re-created each year in our schools. One group of students learns skills and confidence and is prepared for their future, while other students learn their place (at the bottom) in a stratified and difficult economic system.

Of the 11.5 million poor children living below the official poverty line—39.8 percent of all African American children, 32.2 percent of all Latino children, 17.1 percent of all Asian children, 38.8 percent of Native American children, 12.5 percent of all white children—most attend underfunded, poverty-stricken schools. Students in these schools learn that society does not choose to provide them with decent school buildings, computers, counselors, and well-prepared teachers or to open interesting career paths for them.

In most of our major urban centers, a new majority of students has emerged—one composed of diverse people of color: African-Americans, Latinos, Asians, Pacific Islanders, multi-racial kids, and many more. But, in the face of this dramatic shift, the population of teachers remains over 78 percent European American. This division would not be so much a cause for concern except that, according to the 2000 Reading Report Card of the National Center for Educational Statistics, nationally, while 40 percent of white students are proficient in reading in the 4th grade, only 12 percent of black students, 16 percent of Hispanic students and 17 percent of Native American students are proficient. The achievement gap in math scores is equally stark.

The gaps between groups remained relatively unchanged during the 1990s, a decade in which presidents, governors, mayors and legislators all made promises about "school reform." Meanwhile, the longitudinal studies of achievement in the National Reading Report Card demonstrate that, after 20 years of announcements, programs, and pronouncements, achievement levels of US children remain remarkably stable and remarkably unequal.

A Crisis of Inequality

We do not have a general education crisis in the nation: we have a crisis for black, Latino, and some Asian and poor white kids. We are not providing the children of the new majorities with, in W.E.B. Du Bois' words, "a fair start which will equip them with such an array of facts and such an attitude toward truth that they can have a real chance to judge what the world is and what its greater minds have thought it might be."

As David Berliner and Bruce Biddle demonstrated well in *The Manufactured Crisis* (1995), schools for middle-class kids—black, Latino, Asian and European-American—fundamentally fulfill their purposes. But the schools for poor African-American, Latino and European-American children fail. And while this failure affects all poor children, it disproportionately impacts the children of African-Americans, Latinos and Asians. Fully half of all their children are in failing schools. Not 10 percent, not 20 percent, but over 50 percent of these children are being failed.

The problem is not race: there is no intellectually defensible evidence of differences in learning abilities by race. The problem is racism. Racism is developed and strengthened in the continuation of radically unequal learning conditions.

Schools are more segregated by race today than they have been for decades. A close look at the *de facto* segregated urban schools serving people of color reveals, for example, that we have the greatest number of teachers without appropriate preparation in our lowest performing schools. We have teachers with degrees in social studies and art teaching math. Guess what—the students don't learn as much math as they should. In some urban areas, those teaching out of field approach 40 percent of the total.

We now have significant evidence from New York City, Los Angeles, Houston, and many other major city school districts that we can have an African-American superintendent and staff or a Latino superintendent spend 3–5 years on new programs and leave the district having made little substantive difference in students' test scores. We need to invest in urban schools, provide equal educational opportunities in these schools, and recruit a well-prepared teaching force that begins to reflect the student populations in these schools.

Testing vs. Investment

Rather than invest money in reform, most states have followed the lead of conservative foundations and the [Bill] Clinton and [George W.] Bush administrations and increased emphasis on testing to improve scores. This is the heart of school reform passed by the Bush regime in PL 107-110, the misnamed No Child Left Behind Act.[1]

In California, it's the Academic Performance Index; in Texas, the Academic Excellence Indicator system; in Illinois, the Illinois Standards Assessment Systems; and in Massachusetts, the MCAS [Massachusetts Comprehensive Assessment System]. What you will find when looking at the scores in each of these systems is—surprise!—schools with high concentrations of students in poverty have very low academic performance rankings. We are spending millions of dollars to find out what we already know rather than to improve the schools.

Students of Color Get Less

States with Largest Per-Student Funding Gaps and U.S. Average

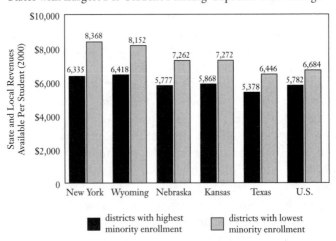

Source: Department of Education and U.S. Census Bureau.

---

1. This act, signed into law in 2001, enacts a number of educational reforms emphasizing scientifically proven teaching methods, expanded parental options, and increased local control of schools.

One would think that we could all agree that children ought to be able to attend public schools that are safe, where gangs and narcotics are not common, where roofs don't leak and plaster doesn't fall from the ceilings. We ought to be able to at least assure our students that the toilets work and fresh water is available. But the *Williams v. California* suit and the Campaign for Fiscal Equity decision in New York clearly show we cannot.

The *Williams* complaint alleges:

> Tens of thousands of children attending public schools located throughout the State of California are being deprived of basic educational opportunities available to more privileged children attending the majority of the State's public schools. State law requires students to attend school. Yet all too many California school children must go to school without trained teachers, necessary educational supplies, classrooms, or seats in classrooms. Students attempt to learn in schools that lack functioning heating or air conditioning systems, that lack sufficient numbers of functional toilets, and that are infested with vermin, including rats, mice, and cockroaches. These appalling conditions in California public schools have persisted for years and have worsened over time.

A fundamental purpose of schools is to prepare future citizens to be stakeholders in society. Public schools are one of the few institutions designed to produce a public, civic community. Schools distribute knowledge. Unequal schools distribute knowledge unequally. When schools distribute knowledge unequally, as they do, they contribute to the social stratification of the economy and the decline of democratic opportunity. Schools do not exist in a vacuum. They are not isolated from their neighborhoods and communities. Inequality in schooling reflects inequality in society.

The Need for a Political Decision

Most parents care about their kids. And parents in urban areas are increasingly angered, offended, and frustrated when public officials refuse to offer a decent opportunity for their children. Some see a racial conspiracy; some blame teachers' unions. Many have given up on democracy and public life and turned to cynicism. Others have been sold on vouchers as an alternative.

So, while schools should be a site for building democracy and equal opportunity, this opportunity can only be created with significant new investment in schools in low-income areas. Investment requires a political decision. Our elected officials, both New Democrats and Republicans, have refused to make this decision each year in most local, state, and federal budgets. As state after state faces the current budget crisis, they are cutting education funding rather than improving funding.

The persistence of inadequate, unsafe, and disruptive conditions clearly indicates that voters and elected officials accept the failure of many of our children, particularly the failure of students of color in urban areas. Although a few districts have improved, and many dedicated teachers continue to struggle against the scandal of urban public schooling, individual efforts are not enough. We need substantial and effective reform.

Research summarized by the Education Trust (www.edtrust.org) and my own experience working with teachers in urban schools for over thirty years lead me to conclude that we know how to improve these schools. I explain many of the details in my book *Choosing Democracy: A Practical Guide to Multicultural Education.*

Improving these schools will cost a great deal of money. We would have to spend as much on the poor kids in the cities as we spend on the middle-class kids in the suburbs. The testing and accountability models presently popular with politicians will not work. And the privatization models being tried in Philadelphia and elsewhere will fail.

A Choice Between Two Futures

Schools can continue as they are. One segment of the society will be well educated and prosperous, and another segment will fail. The schools would continue to serve to train some workers for subservience and to maintain and extend the current racial divisions, which permit the political domination of the corporate ruling class. The economic crisis for working people and people of color will continue to accelerate.

Alternatively, schools can be transformed into places where all students, rich, middle-class and poor, receive compelling, interesting education. Such democratic reform would engage teachers and their unions as equal, trusted, respected partners in progress. Authentic school reform, which requires both teacher union and teacher participation, could play a major role in healing a divided nation. The challenge is both pedagogical and political.

Periodical Bibliography

The following articles have been selected to supplement the diverse views presented in this chapter.

Tom Bethell	"Why the Teachers Can't Be Trusted," *American Spectator*, March/April 2003.
Ronald Brownstein	"Is U.S. Still a Nation at Risk?" *Liberal Opinion Week*, May 26, 2003.
Michael Cardman	"Education Played Role in U.S. Economic Expansion," *Education Daily*, September 16, 2003.
Chester Hartman with Alison Leff	"High Classroom Turnover: How Children Get Left Behind," *Poverty and Race*, May/June 2002.
Daniel Henninger	"Doing the Numbers on Public Schools Adds Up to Zero," *Wall Street Journal*, May 2, 2003.
James B. Hunt Jr.	"Unrecognized Progress," *Education Next*, Spring 2003.
Kenneth Jost	"Grade Inflation," *CQ Researcher*, June 7, 2002.
Terry Keleher and Tammy Johnson	"Confronting Institutional Racism," *Leadership*, March 2001.
Sandra Mathison	"Bribes for Tests," *Z Magazine*, July/August 2003.
Paul E. Peterson	"Ticket to Nowhere," *Education Next*, Spring 2003.
Scott P. Richert	"'Think of the Children!': The Failure of Public Education," *Chronicles*, May 2002.
Phyllis Schlafly	"Leaving More Children Behind," *Human Events*, October 27, 2003.
Christine Sleeter and Peter McLaren	"The Origins of Multiculturalism," *Rethinking Schools*, Fall 2000.
Abigail Thernstrom	"Education's Division Problem," *Los Angeles Times*, November 13, 2003.
Roger H. Weaver	"Real Test Is, Did the Kids Learn to Think?" *Los Angeles Times*, November 5, 2003.
G.E. Zuriff	"Is Racial and Ethnic Diversity Educationally Beneficial?" *World & I*, August 2002.

CHAPTER 2

Are Alternatives to Public Education Viable?

Chapter Preface

Typically, a student enrolled in the U.S. public school system is assigned to a local school by the district. In recent years, however, a growing number of states have enacted "school choice" programs, which allow students to attend schools other than the designated neighborhood school. These programs generally follow one of three models: district-wide plans, which allow parents to select a public school within their district; statewide plans, which permit students to attend public schools outside their home districts; and private school plans, which enable parents to use public funds to send their children to private and parochial schools.

Private school models for school choice, also known as voucher plans, are the most controversial. Proponents argue that vouchers grant low-income families the freedom to take their children out of poorly run public schools and send them to high-quality private schools—an option formerly available only to the wealthy. As activist Alveda King maintains, this kind of school choice will "alleviate [educational] inequality [and] restore parents' and children's civil rights." Critics, however, contend that voucher programs infringe on church-state separation because state funds are often used to pay tuitions at religious schools. Many are especially concerned that taxpayers may end up financing schools that conflict with their beliefs. As former Los Angeles teacher Leonce Gaiter puts it, "Will Jews be forced to underwrite . . . schools that hold Judaism to be a second-class religion? Will gay and lesbian Americans pay for classes teaching that they are sinners deserving of any ill that befalls them?"

In December 2000 an Ohio appeals court addressed such a question in a case involving a school choice program in the city of Cleveland, concluding that government-sponsored scholarships that paid for tuition at sectarian schools violated the constitutional separation of church and state. The ruling was appealed to the U.S. Supreme Court by the state of Ohio as well as by a group of voucher supporters and religious schools participating in the program. In its history-making 2002 decision, the Supreme Court ruled in favor of vouchers, declaring that Cleveland's program did not favor religion over nonreligion since participants can choose among public schools, charter schools (publicly funded schools run by private groups), and religious and secular private schools. As long as choice is allowed and decisions are made by parents—not by the government—public funds may flow to parochial schools without infringing on church-state separation, the Court asserted.

While voucher supporters hailed the Court's decision as a major success, the controversy over school choice is far from over. According to a recent Gallup Poll, 62 percent of Americans oppose allowing parents to choose a private school at public expense, and 76 percent of teachers do not support voucher programs. Moreover, in September 2002, a state judge struck down Florida's school voucher system, arguing that Florida's constitution explicitly prohibits *any* public funding of church schools or other sectarian organizations. Since many states have similarly specific laws banning the transfer of public money to religious institutions, the voucher debate is likely to continue as more cities consider the option of school choice.

In the following chapter, commentators continue this discussion about school vouchers and about alternatives to the mainstream public education system, including home schooling and single-sex schools.

| "*Why not give vouchers to poor and minority parents so they [can] choose the best education for their children?*"

Tuition Vouchers Can Improve Education

Clint Bolick

Many proponents of school choice support the use of vouchers—state-funded tuition grants—that allow low-income parents to use public money to send their children to private or parochial schools. In the following viewpoint Clint Bolick argues in favor of vouchers, contending that this form of government aid gives poor and minority parents the opportunity to take their children out of dysfunctional public schools and send them to high-quality schools that they otherwise could not afford. The voucher movement should be seen as a civil rights struggle—as a means for inner-city students to become educated, productive adults, Bolick maintains. Moreover, he concludes, public education will improve as it encounters competition from schools that accept vouchers. Bolick is vice president of the Institute for Justice and the author of *Voucher Wars: Waging the Legal Battle over School Choice*.

As you read, consider the following questions:

1. What did the U.S. Supreme Court decide in the 1925 case of *Pierce v. Society of Sisters*, according to the author?
2. Why do suburban public schools and inner-city private schools produce good academic outcomes, according to Bolick?

Clint Bolick, "The Key to Closing the Minority Schooling Gap: School Choice," *The American Enterprise*, vol. 14, April/May 2003, p. 30. Copyright © 2003 by the American Enterprise Institute for Public Policy Research. Reproduced by permission of *The American Enterprise*, a magazine of Politics, Business, and Culture. On the Web at www.TAEmag.com.

In a nation supposedly committed to free enterprise, consumer choice, and equal educational opportunities, school choice should be routine. That it is not demonstrates the clout of those dedicated to preserving the government's monopoly over public education. To listen to the education establishment, one would think that school choice is a radical, scary, alien concept. Indeed, the defenders of the status quo have convinced many voters that school choice is a threat to American society.

But school choice is not threatening, and it is not new. To the contrary, it is the norm in most modern nations. Even in the U.S., non-government schools have long played a key educational role, often using public funds. America's college system—the world's envy—is built on school choice: Students can use the G.I. Bill, Pell Grants, and other forms of government aid to attend either public or private schools, including religious institutions. At the other end of the age spectrum, parents of preschoolers can use child care vouchers in private and religious settings. And under federal law, tens of thousands of disabled elementary and high school age children receive schooling in private schools at public expense. It is only mainstream K-12 schools in which the government commands a monopoly over public funds.

The History of School Choice

Thomas Paine, the most prescient of our founding fathers, is credited with first suggesting a voucher system in the United States. He wanted an educated, enlightened citizenry, but the idea that the government should operate schools was an alien concept to him and his generation. Instead, Paine proposed providing citizens with financial support that they could use to purchase education in private schools.

The great portion of early American "public" education took place in private schools. Even when states started creating government schools, the teachers often were ministers. The concept of "separation of church and state" is not in the U.S. Constitution, and was certainly never applied to education.

In 1869, Vermont adopted a school choice program for communities that did not build their own public schools, and Maine followed suit in 1873. To this day, both states will pay tuition for children to attend private schools, or public schools in neighboring communities. In Vermont, 6,500 children from 90 towns attend private schools at government expense; in Maine, 5,600 children from 55 towns do so. Those programs, in existence for more than a century and a quarter, have not destroyed the local public schools; to the contrary, both states boast a well-educated population.

The Rise of Catholic Schools

But the goal of universal common schooling, fueled by the ideas of Horace Mann, helped make government schools the norm in the late nineteenth century. Thereafter, private schools typically served two groups: the elite, and those seeking a religious immersion different from the Protestant theology that dominated public schools. The latter, of course, were primarily Catholic immigrants.

The rise of Catholic schools bitterly annoyed Protestant public school advocates like Senator James Blaine (R-ME). Blaine struck back in 1876. His proposed amendment to the U.S. Constitution to prohibit any government aid to religious schools came just short of securing passage in Congress. His allies, however, lobbied state legislatures and succeeded in attaching "Blaine amendments" to approximately 37 state constitutions which prohibited expenditure of public funds in "support" of sectarian (i.e., Catholic) schools. Anti-Catholic bigotry crested in an Oregon law, secured by the Ku Klux Klan, which required all children to attend government schools.

In the landmark 1925 decision *Pierce v. Society of Sisters*, the U.S. Supreme Court struck down that Oregon law, declaring that "The fundamental theory of liberty upon which all governments in this Union repose excludes any general power of the State to standardize its children by forcing them to accept instruction from public teachers only. The child is not the mere creature of the State; those who nurture him and direct his destiny have the right, coupled with the high duty, to recognize and prepare him for additional obligations." This principle of parental sovereignty remains a cornerstone of American law today. Though it remains constantly under attack, it continues to keep private educational options (among other rights) open to parents.

The Modern Case for School Vouchers

The modern case for school vouchers was first made by the Nobel laureate economist Milton Friedman in 1955. Instead of providing education as a monopoly supplier, Friedman suggested, government should just finance it. Every child would be given a voucher redeemable at a school of the parent's choice, public or private. Schools would compete to attract the vouchers. Friedman's proposal contained two insights that formed the intellectual foundations of the contemporary school choice movement: that parents, rather than government, should decide where children attend school, and that the economic rules which yield good services and products are not suspended at the schoolhouse door.

Constructive Competition

An initiative of choice through vouchers or tax credits, with few restrictions on private schools, not only will give children access to a better education, it will unleash the power of constructive competition that will lead to dramatically improved outcomes in the future. A voucher or tax credit of $5,000 or more per student would give families the clout they need as consumers. There already are many affordable high quality private schools available on the market and, once they are allowed to compete on a level playing field with government schools, many more will come into operation. . . . It is imperative not to delay further, but to implement school choice reforms as soon as possible.

David F. Salisbury, *USA Today Magazine*, November 2003.

Support for school choice began to expand and diversify in the 1970s, when two liberal Berkeley law professors, Jack Coons and Steven Sugarman, began to consider school choice as a means of delivering educational equity. If forced busing plans had failed, Coons and Sugarman argued, why not give vouchers to poor and minority parents so they could choose the best education for their children? Coons and Sugarman adapted Friedman's proposal to their own ends: While Friedman advocated universal vouchers, Coons and Sugarman wanted to target them to disadvantaged populations. Friedman preferred a lightly regulated system, while Coons and Sugarman called for substantial government oversight.

Still, there was the beginning of an alliance between freedom-seeking conservatives on the one hand and equality-seeking liberals on the other. That alliance eventually made the school choice programs of the 1990s a reality.

The main force generating support for vouchers, however, was the alarming decline in urban public schools. During the 1960s and 1970s, most urban public schools were ruined. Whites and middle-class blacks fled to the suburbs, leaving poor and mostly minority populations in rapidly worsening city public schools.

The problems of urban public schools were connected to a broader decline in public education. The 1983 study *A Nation at Risk* warned that large doses of mediocrity and failure had crept into American public schools. Meanwhile, starting in the 1980s, social scientists like James Coleman began showing that private and religious schools were succeeding in educating the very same poor, minority schoolchildren that government schools were failing. Many corroborating studies followed.

A Supportive Study

Also helping set the stage for a school choice movement was the 1990 Brookings Institution study by John Chubb and Terry Moe, *Politics, Markets & America's Schools.* Chubb and Moe set out to discover why suburban public schools and inner-city private schools generally produced good academic outcomes, while inner-city public schools were disasters. They found that whereas the first two types of schools were characterized by strong leaders with a clear mission and a high degree of responsiveness to parents, inner-city schools were not. Instead, urban public school districts were run by bloated bureaucracies whose principal constituencies were not parents, but politicians and unions.

A crucial factor distinguishing the successful and unsuccessful schools was the element of choice: Suburban parents could send their children to private schools, or move to different communities, if they were dissatisfied with their public schools. Private schools, obviously, were entirely dependent on satisfied parents. But inner-city public school parents were captives: They had no choice except to send their children to whatever the local government school offered. In school districts with tens or hundreds of thousands of students, they were powerless to do anything about the system.

Introducing choice in inner-city public schools, Chubb and Moe concluded—particularly giving parents the power to exit the public system altogether—would force the bureaucracy to respond to its customers rather than to politicians and special-interest groups. These findings created a scholarly foundation for school choice as a way not merely of helping children in failing government schools, but also as an essential prerequisite for reforming public school systems.

A Sophisticated Movement

When the current school choice movement started to come together a decade or two ago, its leading protagonists could have met comfortably in a telephone booth. In an amazingly short period, it has grown into a sophisticated, passionate, and ecumenical movement. There are philanthropists, activists, public officials, clergy, lawyers, and parents, all willing to put aside ideological differences in pursuit of a common cause.

The movement's core argument is that parents, not government, should have the primary responsibility and power to determine where and how their children are educated. That this basic principle should require a vicious fight is testimony to the strength, determination, and ferocity of the reactionary forces defending today's educational status quo. Teacher unions, which form the cornerstone of our education establishment, are the most powerful special-interest group in America today. At the national level, they essentially own the Democratic Party. At the state level, they wield enormous influence over elected officials in both parties. At the local level, they frequently control school boards. They and their education allies have dedicated all the resources at their disposal to defeat meaningful school choice anywhere it has presented itself.

For the education establishment, this battle is about preserving their monopolistic vise grip on American schooling. For parents—and our society—the stakes are much higher.

Nearly 50 years after *Brown v. Board of Education*,[1] vast numbers of black and Hispanic children do not graduate from high school. Many of those who do still lack the most basic skills needed for even entry-level jobs. As a result, many children in inner-city schools wind up on welfare or in jail. Children who most need the compensations of a quality education are instead relegated to dysfunctional schools. In climbing out of this morass we should not worry about whether a particular reform is too radical; we should worry about whether it is radical enough.

The school choice movement is not only a crusade to improve American education. It is also a true civil rights struggle. It is critical to the real lives of real people. The system has written off many of the people who most need choice—both the parents and their children. Minority citizens may be offered welfare payments, or racial preferences, but little is done to help them become productive, self-supporting citizens. Government schools and their liberal patrons implicitly assume that low-income children are incapable of learning. With little expected of these children, that becomes a self-fulfilling prophecy.

An Alternative to Failure

Meanwhile, conditions are different in most inner-city private schools. Not because they have greater resources than their public school counterparts (they typically have far fewer), or because they are selective (they usually accept all applicants), but rather because the operating philosophy is markedly different. At non-government schools, parents are not discouraged from involvement, they are required to play a role in the school and in their children's education. The children are expected to behave. They are expected to achieve. And research shows that they do.

Ultimately, we want school choice programs that are large and accessible enough to give government schools a serious run for their money. But initially, even a small program—publicly or privately funded—can begin to introduce inner-

1. the 1954 Supreme Court case in which racial segregation in schools was declared unconstitutional

city parents to the previously unknown concept that there is an alternative to failure. That creates a constituency for a larger program.

Any functioning program, no matter how small, will change the debate from one about hypotheticals to one about realities. When we can show that competition helps public schools, and that families are choosing good schools rather than, say, witchcraft schools, we can begin to debunk the myths of choice adversaries. In Milwaukee, where school choice has been pioneered, public opinion polls show that support for choice is stronger the closer one is to the program. Not only inner-city parents but also suburban parents now support school choice there.

Actual experience has shown that school choice programs do not, "skim the cream" of students, as our detractors like to say, leaving only hard cases in the public schools. Instead (not surprisingly), school choice programs usually attract children who are experiencing academic or disciplinary problems in government schools. Many such children are on a downward trajectory. Just arresting that trajectory is an accomplishment, even if it doesn't show up immediately in improved test scores.

Academic research by Harvard's Paul Peterson and others shows that academic gains are modest in the first year or two of a school choice program, and begin to accelerate afterward. Longitudinal studies tracking choice students over many years seem likely to find higher high school graduation and college enrollment rates, plus other measures of success. If that happens, the debate over the desirability of school choice will be over. The pioneers of school choice will have shown how to rescue individuals from otherwise dark futures, as well as how to force our larger system of public education to improve itself for the good of all students.

"[Vouchers] mean [that] private schools get public dollars yet don't have to be accountable to the public."

Tuition Vouchers Will Not Improve Education

Part I: Barbara Miner; Part II: Alain Jehlen

The authors of the following two-part viewpoint contend that government money should not be used to pay for tuitions at private schools. In Part I, Barbara Miner argues that tuition vouchers are a bad idea because the private schools that take voucher students are not held to the same standards of accountability that public schools are. Moreover, since private schools tend to choose the best students, the needy and more difficult students would be left behind in public schools that are losing funding. In Part II, Alain Jehlen maintains that there is no evidence that students in voucher programs do better academically than public school students. Miner is managing editor of *Rethinking Schools*, a grassroots education journal. Jehlen is a staff writer for *NEA Today*, a journal published by the National Education Association.

As you read, consider the following questions:
1. In Miner's opinion, what is one of the greatest ironies about school vouchers?
2. According to Jehlen, what research flaws undermine the claim that vouchers improve student performance?

I

The principal was being fired, teachers were leaving, the school was in upheaval. At the time, I was a reporter for the *Milwaukee Journal* covering a parents' meeting discussing the controversy.

I never made it to the meeting. Lawyers stood in my way and said it was a private school and reporters were not welcome. End of discussion.

I was enraged—but found out the lawyers were right. Shutting a reporter out of a parents' meeting is against the law in Milwaukee public schools. But private schools get to operate by different rules.

I was reminded of this incident recently when the Wisconsin Supreme Court upheld the constitutionality of Milwaukee's voucher program. For now, at least, low-income students in Milwaukee will be able to use public vouchers to attend private and religious schools in the city. The decision has national implications; publicly funded vouchers for private schools are at the top of the Republican education agenda. If vouchers are not yet an issue in your state, wait a month or two.

Legal Is Not Necessarily Good

In the controversy over whether vouchers for religious schools violate the constitutional separation of church and state, an equally important issue is often obscured. Just because something is legal doesn't mean it is good public policy. It is legal, for example, to sell off public parks and close public playgrounds and swimming pools. But it is a stupid idea.

It's not mere coincidence that the term "private" is so often followed by the phrase, "Keep Out!" Private schools, like private roads, private beaches and private country clubs, don't have to be accountable to the public. They also get to keep out those they don't want. That's why they are called "private."

What does it mean when private schools get public dollars yet don't have to be accountable to the public? Under the recently upheld legislation, for instance, private schools in Milwaukee's voucher program:

- Do not have to obey the state's open meetings and records laws.

- Do not have to hire certified teachers or even require a college degree.
- Do not have to release information on employee wages or benefits.
- Do not have to provide data such as test scores, attendance figures, or suspension and drop-out rates. In fact, the legislation expanding vouchers to include religious schools specifically eliminated the requirement that the State Superintendent of Schools conduct annual performance evaluations of voucher schools.

Regulations governing private schools are so weak that it is harder to get a liquor license or set up a corner gas station in Milwaukee than it is to start a private school.

The private schools can also weed out "undesirable" students and families. For example, they can set admission requirements and expel or suspend students with no due process. Most important, they do not have to accept students with special educational needs—which accounts for nearly 15% of Milwaukee public school students, and the most expensive, most difficult to educate. Further, some private schools require parents to pay hundreds of dollars in "fees," above and beyond the voucher-supported tuition.

Unanswered Questions

There are also unanswered legal questions. Religious schools can legally fire teachers who violate religious principles—such as gay teachers, divorced teachers, or teachers who support the right to abortion—and expel students who support them. Will religious schools who receive vouchers also be able to teach that the non-baptized will go to hell, that the Jews killed Christ, or that there is no God but Allah?

What about desegregation? One of Milwaukee's dirty little secrets is that white parents often use private schools to get around desegregation efforts. In Milwaukee, for example, the public schools are 60% African-American. At Divine Savior/Holy Angels and at Pius XI, two prominent Catholic high schools in the city, only 3% of the students are African American. Nor are those figures atypical.

One of the greatest ironies is that at a time when the state is requiring more accountability from public schools, the private voucher schools can ignore the call for standards. In Wisconsin, as in most states, private schools are exempt from statewide standardized tests. After all, the argument goes, they are "private" schools.

Sargent. © 2002 by *The Austin American-Statesman*. Reproduced by permission of Universal Press Syndicate.

Up to 15,000 children in Milwaukee [can] use public money to attend private and religious schools. . . . With the voucher worth almost $5,000 per pupil, that means that as much as $75 million in taxpayers' money will be taken from the Milwaukee public schools and given to schools that do not have to meet minimum requirements of public accountability.

It may be legal. But is it a good idea?

Think about it. Vouchers are coming your way.

II

[In 2002], the nine Supreme Court justices are scheduled to decide whether vouchers—public money going to private K-12 schools—violate the U.S. Constitution. Voucher supporters have for years been saying private schools can do a much better job than public schools. But the public has been skeptical, recently defeating voucher referenda in California and Michigan by overwhelming margins. [In August 2001], the

General Accounting Office (GAO) took a hard look at the evidence. Their conclusion: There's no valid evidence that vouchers help students learn.

Where are vouchers now in effect?

The program before the Supreme Court is in Cleveland, Ohio. As of June 2000, roughly 3,400 Cleveland students had vouchers. About 97 percent of them were going to religious schools. According to the GAO, "the maximum voucher amount ($2,250 for low-income students) established by the Ohio legislature at the beginning of the voucher program appears to have limited the program primarily to low-tuition religious schools." The use of tax money to support religious schools is one of the issues before the Supreme Court.[1]

Milwaukee, Wisconsin, has a larger program with 7,600 children as of 2000. Florida has a small voucher program. Maine and Vermont have long-standing programs but only for students in rural districts where there is no age-appropriate public school, and the private schools must be secular.

Research on Vouchers

What is the GAO?

The General Accounting Office is the investigative arm of Congress. It conducts a wide range of studies on public policy issues.

What did the GAO report say about vouchers and student learning?

The GAO reviewed studies of test scores for students from Cleveland and Milwaukee, comparing children in voucher programs with other children who were in the public schools. GAO found no evidence that children in voucher programs do better.

The researchers based their report on studies commissioned by state education departments in Ohio and Wisconsin. The GAO referred to these studies as "contracted evaluations."

The report says: "The contracted evaluations of voucher

---

1. In June 2002 the Supreme Court ruled that Cleveland's voucher program did not violate the Constitution.

students' academic achievement in Cleveland and Milwaukee found little or no difference in voucher and public school students' performance."

What about researchers who claim that vouchers do work?

The GAO report said their studies did not meet the standards of good social science because they did not use adequate controls. To tell whether students benefit from vouchers, researchers must compare children who use vouchers with similar children in public schools. GAO found that pro-voucher researchers failed to do this.

Why are there conflicting claims about the effects of vouchers?

It is very difficult to conduct valid, objective research on "social engineering" experiments like vouchers because people can't be treated like guinea pigs—they can't be assigned randomly to one program or another, don't necessarily stay in the program once they start, and can't be forced to cooperate with researchers even if they do stay.

In Cleveland and Milwaukee, a high percentage of families did not return survey questionnaires. Were these families similar to those that did return questionnaires? Some children went to private schools on vouchers but then left. Could some of them have left because they did badly there?

Some students were offered vouchers but turned them down and stayed in the public schools. Others left the public schools when they learned they would not get vouchers. Perhaps these were children whose parents planned to put them in private schools all along.

In addition, researchers were unable to get some of the test score data they needed.

In all these situations, researchers had to make assumptions about the missing or possibly biased data. GAO concluded that the different study conclusions were due to different sets of assumptions that researchers made.

However, even the most pro-voucher researchers have limited their claims of success to certain groups of students at certain grade levels. After a much-hyped report on privately funded vouchers in three cities, one of the chief investigators took the highly unusual step of warning publicly that the person in charge of the study was going beyond the data to put a positive spin on vouchers.

Strategies for Learning

What are some proven strategies for helping students learn?

There is solid evidence based on several well-controlled, long-term studies that children learn better in small classes with well-trained, experienced teachers. Small classes appear to be especially beneficial for low-income children, the same children whom voucher proponents claim to be trying to help.

What is NEA [National Education Association] doing about vouchers?

NEA and its state affiliates are playing a leading role in opposing vouchers. At the national, state, and local levels, NEA lobbyists and members educate policy-makers and opinion leaders about the strengths of public education. . . .

Most important, NEA works to build public confidence in the public schools by improving schools for all students.

> "*For Christians who sense God's call to move their children to a private school, there will finally be a genuine option.*"

Tuition Vouchers Promote Religious Liberty

David Neff

The 2002 Supreme Court decision upholding school vouchers is a boon for religious parents who want more control over their children's education, argues David Neff in the following viewpoint. Now that voucher programs have Court approval, the long-running monopoly of antireligious public schools will eventually end. Parents will finally have a genuine opportunity to send their children to high-quality schools that reflect their ideals and values, the author asserts. Neff is the editor of *Christianity Today*, a monthly magazine containing news and editorials reflecting an evangelical Christian perspective.

As you read, consider the following questions:
1. According to the author, what helped to energize the movement for government-run schools?
2. Why do many Americans resent the public-school monopoly, in Neff's view?
3. According to this viewpoint, what percentage of students drops out of public school before the twelfth grade?

David Neff, "Breaking Up a Monopoly: The Supreme Court Has Put Parents Back in Charge of Their Children's Education," *Christianity Today*, vol. 46, August 5, 2002, p. 28. Copyright © 2002 by David Neff. Reproduced by permission.

The U.S. Supreme Court blew out the cornerstone of racial segregation with *Brown v. Board of Education*, its monumental decision in 1954. The Court's new [2002] decision in *Zelman v. Simmons-Harris* will do the same to state-sponsored anti-religious bias.

The 5-4 Court majority upheld a Cleveland voucher program that gives tax dollars mostly to impoverished parents, who in turn can use that money at any participating school: public, private, or parochial. With this decision, the Court has redefined the meaning of public education in America and effectively ended the monopoly of secular government schools. It's about time.

The ideas of Thomas Jefferson, Horace Mann, and others laid the intellectual foundation for a government-run school system 160 years ago, but religious and ethnic prejudice energized that movement. When European Catholic immigrants began pouring into Boston and New York in the 1840s, local and state governments were troubled—what would happen to "America" if such people, most of whom attended Catholic schools, were encouraged to keep their culture? Governments decided to organize schooling to promote a common culture—meaning, in essence, a white, Anglo-Saxon, Protestant culture. They defined Catholic schools, among others, as private, "sectarian" affairs undeserving of public support.

Not until the 1960s, when the secularism of Thomas Dewey and other educational theorists made its way into curriculum across the country, did Protestants begin to feel Catholics' pain. This was no sinister plot, but the logical outcome of a school system run by the government in a democratic society: The perceived assumptions and prejudices of most Americans became the basis for making decisions about what should go on in the public classroom.

And when educational bureaucrats get into their minds some notion they imagine is the wave of the future (e.g., the full acceptance of homosexuality), the system ends up teaching a pagan approach to ethics as normative for all students. In short, our current system seems hardly conducive to respecting the rights and desires of religious minorities. The system undermines one of the very principles it seeks to promote: genuine pluralism. It is no wonder that many Americans resent the educational monopoly.

Most parents instinctually understand that they (not the State) are responsible for training their children (Prov. 22:6; Deut. 6:4-9). They also understand that education has to be founded on a coherent worldview. To have students learning relativistic secularism in the classroom makes it that much more difficult to impart transcendent values at home, and it teaches children to compartmentalize, rather than integrate, their knowledge (as if one set of intellectual rules apply at school and another at home).

This monopoly has other problems. It's no secret that too many of the nation's public schools are failing to provide an adequate education for the most vulnerable children. Since 1983, over 13 million children have reached the 12th grade not knowing how to read at a basic level. Over 27 million have reached their senior year unable to do basic math—not to mention the 30 percent who drop out of school before the 12th grade.

Cleveland's situation a few years ago was telling: only 1 of 10 Cleveland ninth-graders could pass a basic proficiency exam, two-thirds of high school students dropped out before graduation, and the district as a whole could not meet any of the 18 state standards for minimal performance. Inner-city parents thought that private schools of whatever religious stripe could do better. The point of vouchers was simple: to give parents genuine choice—to allow some of their tax dollars to support schools that they believed would meet their educational goals. The Supreme Court agreed: "Our holding thus rested not on whether few or many recipients chose to expend government aid at a religious school but, rather, on whether recipients generally were empowered to direct the aid to schools or institutions of their own choosing."

The Supreme Court has implicitly recognized that in a democratic, pluralistic society, a government monopoly on public education sometimes leads to horrific educational consequences and resentment among students and parents—and that it doesn't have to be this way. Parents can have genuine choices.

Involved Learners

Will a school system based on free parental choice turn American society toward scholastic feudalism, each interest group having its own school, insistently separate from the rest of society?

Apparently it doesn't work that way. As sociologist Christian Smith writes,

> Recent survey data from the U.S. Department of Education show that Catholic, Protestant, and nonreligious private schooling and homeschooling families are consistently more involved in a wide spectrum of civic activities than are families of public school children. From voting to volunteering to visiting the local library, private and homeschooling families are very much out in their communities and involved in the affairs of public life. Private schooling, it turns out, is anything but privatizing.

A new era is dawning in education. School voucher programs already exist in Wisconsin, Florida, Vermont, and Maine. In [2002] alone, legislatures in 12 states considered parental choice proposals. More states will no doubt give such proposals a fresh look.

We don't foresee masses of Christians withdrawing from

the school systems. In fact, we hope this doesn't happen. Many schools would be the poorer for Christians' withdrawal. But for Christians who sense God's call to move their children to a private school, there will finally be a genuine option in a handful of states. If reason and genuine diversity prevail, that option will spread to all states.

"Government has no business legislating for or against religions and cannot force taxpayers to support religious institutions."

Tuition Vouchers Threaten Religious Liberty

Charles Levendosky

In the following viewpoint journalist Charles Levendosky maintains that the 2002 Supreme Court decision upholding school voucher programs defies the constitutional separation of state and religion. The Bill of Rights explicitly prohibits the use of tax dollars to support religious institutions, he points out. Vouchers, state-funded tuition grants that allow parents to send their children to private or parochial schools, endanger religious liberty because they can force taxpayers to fund religious organizations they despise; moreover, religious institutions face the prospect of government scrutiny and interference when they accept state aid. Before his death in 2004, Levendosky was an editor for the *Casper (Wyoming) Star-Tribune*.

As you read, consider the following questions:

1. In the author's view, why would Thomas Jefferson and James Madison have been appalled by the Supreme Court decision upholding school vouchers?
2. What was the focus of Justice William Rehnquist's argument in favor of school vouchers, according to Levendosky?
3. According to the author, what was the Supreme Court's decision in the 1947 case of *Everson v. Board of Education of Ewing*?

Charles Levendosky, "Voucher Decision Sidesteps Constitution," *Progressive Populist*, vol. 8, August 1–15, 2002, p. 21. Copyright © 2002 by *Progressive Populist*. Reproduced by permission of the author.

Chief Justice William Rehnquist can now retire from the US Supreme Court, smug in the knowledge that he has helped drive a bulldozer into the wall that separates church and state. He doesn't accept the principle of separation of church and state, which is the core of our religious liberty.

Despite being the high court's top justice, Rehnquist has never been a serious student of constitutional history.

An Untenable Position

Even if one takes the stance that the US Constitution is an evolving document, written in broad enough language to be adapted to changes over time; nevertheless, core principles, like religious liberty, fair trials and freedom of speech, must remain inviolate or the Constitution itself is betrayed.

Based upon constitutional history and jurisprudence, the position taken by Rehnquist, who wrote the opinion for a 5-to-4 majority in the Ohio vouchers case, is untenable. On June 27 [2002], the court's majority upheld Ohio's Pilot Project Scholarship Program which provides taxpayer money as tuition aid for students in the Cleveland City School District (*Zelman, Superintendent of Public Instruction of Ohio v. Simmons-Harris*).

Rehnquist—joined by Justices Sandra Day O'Connor, Antonin Scalia, Anthony Kennedy and Clarence Thomas—wrote that using Ohio taxpayer dollars to support religious schools does not violate the Establishment Clause.

According to court documents, in the 1999–2000 school year more than 3,700 students participated in the scholarship program, and 96% of those students were enrolled in religious schools. Depending upon need, the state provides up to $2,250 for tuition, to be used at participating schools that parents choose.

In his dissent, Justice Stephen Breyer pointed out the school voucher program is a "direct financing to a core function of the church: the teaching of religious truths to young children."

The Founders Would Be Appalled

The two founders most responsible for the religious liberty clauses in the Bill of Rights, James Madison and Thomas

Jefferson, would have been appalled by the court's decision.

In 1785, in response to a bill to levy a tax on Virginians to pay Virginia teachers of the Christian religion, Madison wrote his powerful treatise, "Memorial and Remonstrance Against Religious Assessments." He called the taxpayer bill "a dangerous abuse of power."

The second section of "Memorial and Remonstrance" begins: "Because Religion be exempt from the authority of the Society at large, still less can it be subject to that of the Legislative Body."

In 1779, Thomas Jefferson, in his "Bill for Establishing Religious Freedom in Virginia," wrote, "to compel a man to furnish contributions of money for the propagation of opinions which he disbelieves and abhors, is sinful and tyrannical." And in 1786, the General Assembly of Virginia passed the bill, which states in part: "no man shall be compelled to frequent or support any religious worship, place, or ministry whatsoever."

If there is central meaning to the principle of separation of church and state, as embodied in the Establishment Clause, it is that government has no business legislating for or against religions and cannot force taxpayers to support religious institutions.

Religious liberty does not exist when an unwilling taxpayer is forced to contribute to the religious institutions he or she abhors.

And religious liberty ceases to exist when government intrudes upon religious institutions and their teachings.

Potential Problems

It has been generally ignored that the voucher program allows Ohio education officials to investigate religious schools to determine whether a particular religious doctrine "teaches hatred or advocates lawlessness." Justice Breyer called attention to the fact that state officials can even revoke a religious school's participation in the program if it advocates civil disobedience in response to some social practice or political issue.

The Ohio voucher program pays religious schools to teach children religious truths that some Ohio taxpayers might find offensive or blasphemy. Nonetheless, their tax dollars support those schools. And some religious schools may have their participation revoked by government officials who feel their beliefs are not mainstream. With the high court's blessings, other states may decide to initiate voucher programs, too.

Unprecedented Funding

Vouchers could become vehicles for unprecedented transfers of public funds from public schools to private, parochial ones. Taxpayers may be forced to provide substantial financial support to sectarian religious institutions they abhor (or consider heretical), and religious institutions may find the tenets of their faiths compromised by the government oversight that is likely to accompany government funds. The Cleveland voucher program upheld by the Court, for example, requires private schools accepting vouchers to refrain from preaching religious hatred (a provision that may be broadly construed) and from discriminating against students or teachers on the basis of religion, race or ethnicity.

Wendy Kaminer, *American Prospect*, August 26, 2002.

Understandably in writing the opinion for the majority, Rehnquist doesn't make a constitutional argument. He cannot. Instead Rehnquist makes a social argument. He points out that Cleveland's public school system was in a crisis of unparalleled magnitude. It was among the worst performing school districts in the nation.

A federal court had placed the Cleveland school district under state control. The voucher program was Ohio's strategy to solving the problem. While not dismissing the seriousness of the problems in Cleveland's schools, the attempt to solve them should not be unconstitutional.

A Sham Rationale

The magnitude of the problem is Rehnquist's justification for ducking a constitutional argument. He sidesteps the Establishment Clause by asserting the voucher program is neutral with respect to religion and its direct government aid to religious schools is the result of parents' "own genuine and independent private choice." Therefore, he argues, "the Establishment Clause is not implicated."

This is a sham rationale which has no constitutional foundation. It authorizes what the founders considered an unconstitutional breech of the wall between church and state. And unfortunately, the court's decision encourages and enables further abuses of religious liberty.

The ruling overturns 55 years of the high court's jurisprudence regarding support for religions. In *Everson v. Board of Education of Ewing* (1947) a unanimous court wrote: "No tax in any amount, large or small, can be levied to support any religious activities or institutions, whatever they may be called, or whatever form they may adopt to teach or practice religion."

Everson was never overruled, yet Rehnquist doesn't mention it at all in his decision. He avoids it, just as he avoided a constitutional argument.

This is one of the . . . most shameful and troublesome decisions regarding religious liberty to come out of the Supreme Court in decades. . . .

More than 200 years ago, this nation opted for a constitutional form of government. It isn't always easy to act within the framework of our Constitution, but that's the price we pay to ensure our liberty.

"The home educated score as well as or better [on tests] than those in conventional schools."

Home Schooling Is a Viable Alternative to Public Education

Isabel Lyman

A growing number of families are choosing to educate their children at home. In the following viewpoint Isabel Lyman contends that home schooling is a feasible option for parents who want to ensure a quality education for their children. A variety of home schooling methods and aids are available, she points out, and the freedom afforded by home education presents opportunities for individually tailored instruction, the imparting of religious values, volunteer activities, and creativity. In addition, homeschooled students generally perform well on standardized tests, and the claim that they are poorly socialized is unfounded. Lyman, a mother who homeschools, is the author of *The Homeschooling Revolution*.

As you read, consider the following questions:

1. According to Lyman, what are the top four reasons that parents choose to homeschool?
2. What kinds of educational approaches are adopted by home schooling parents, according to the author?
3. What research does Lyman cite as proof that homeschoolers learn good social and behavioral skills?

Isabel Lyman, "Answers to Homeschool Questions: Knowledgeable Answers to Seven Frequently Asked Questions About Homeschooling Explain the Benefits of Home Education and Dispel Some Typical Misperceptions," *New American*, vol. 18, May 6, 2002, p. 31. Copyright © 2002 by American Opinion Publishing, Inc. Reproduced by permission.

Here are seven of the most frequently asked questions about home education and home educators:

Why do families choose to homeschool?

Dr. Brian Ray of the National Home Education Research Institute offers this on his website: "Increased safety is a main reason for homeschooling (e.g. physical violence, drug and alcohol use, psychological abuse by schools, peer pressure to engage in premarital sexual behaviors)."

In 1996, the Florida Department of Education surveyed 2,245 homeschoolers, and 31 percent of that number returned the survey. Of that group, 42 percent said that dissatisfaction with the public school environment (safety, drugs, adverse peer pressure) was their reason for launching a home education program.

Focusing on homeschooling, my own doctoral dissertation analysis of over 300 newspaper and magazine articles revealed that the top four reasons to bypass conventional schooling were dissatisfaction with the public schools, the desire to freely impart religious values, academic excellence, and the building of stronger family bonds.

Choosing to Homeschool

What types of families choose to homeschool?

Americans of different races, socioeconomic backgrounds, and religions homeschool. Given Americans' penchant for associations, there are national homeschooling support groups for Protestants, Catholics, Jews, Muslims, Mormons, the disabled, and people of color. For instance, Johnson Obamehinti founded Minority Homeschoolers of Texas. His organization promotes home education among ethnic minorities, such as African-Americans, Asians, Hispanics, Jews, Native Americans, and Anglos with adopted minority children.

The Associated Press reported the findings of a U.S. Department of Education report about the "average" homeschooler [in 2001]. The AP story noted, "They are more likely than other students to live with two or more siblings in a two-parent family, with one parent working outside the home. Parents of homeschoolers are, on average, better educated than other parents—a greater percentage have college degrees—though their incomes are about the same. Like most parents, the vast majority of those who homeschool their children earn less than $50,000, and many earn less than $25,000."

Homeschooling has also attracted the "high-profiled" to its ranks. U.S. Senator Rick Santorum (R-Penn.) and Karen, his wife, are the homeschooling parents of six children. Others include Jason Taylor, who plays in the National Football League, and Christina Aguilera, the pop music entertainer.

The Performance of Homeschoolers

How do homeschoolers fare academically?

One measure is how well they perform on standardized tests, like the Stanford Achievement Test or the Iowa Test of Basic Skills. The National Home Education Research Institute notes, "Repeatedly, across the nation, the home educated score as well as or better than those in conventional schools."

The National Merit Scholarship Corporation selected more than 70 homeschooled high school students as semi-finalists in its 1998 competition. There were 137 home-schooled semifinalists chosen in 1999, and 150 in 2000.

Rebecca Sealfon, a 13-year-old homeschooler from Brooklyn, New York, won the 1997 Scripps Howard National Spelling Bee. David Beihl, also 13, of Saluda, South Carolina, won the 1999 National Geography Bee. Finishing second in the 2000 National Geography Bee, George Thampy, a 12-year-old homeschooler from Maryland Heights, Missouri, won the National Spelling Bee for that same year. Homeschooled students were the top three finishers at the 2000 National Spelling Bee, as were three of the ten finalists in the 2001 National Geography Bee. Of the 248 spellers that competed in the 2001 Scripps Howard National Spelling Bee, 25 were schooled at home.

Homeschoolers have graduated from such prestigious institutions as Yale University Law School, the United States Naval Academy, and Mount Holyoke College.

How many homeschoolers are there?

No exact figures exist, but there is a general consensus that homeschoolers comprise at least one percent of the school-aged population of 50 million children. [In 2001] the Department of Education estimated the number at 850,000, based

Imaginative Curricula

Frequently, home-schooling parents design their own curricula. When done right, they can be imaginative and substantial. Kenneth Robinson, a lawyer by training, is one of the rare fathers who stays at home to teach (his wife writes and illustrates children's books in a wing of their pleasant Ware, Massachusetts, home). His self-designed curriculum uses "the best books I think available." Whitney, his 13-year-old daughter, begins her day with pre-algebra math, and then moves on to reading—Arthur Conan Doyle's collected Sherlock Holmes stories and C.S. Lewis's *Mere Christianity* are currently on the plate. Then it's time for logic. "I stress thinking skills and the ability to reason correctly, so we spend time looking at arguments and critiquing them for logical fallacies," Robinson says. In the afternoon, Robinson and his daughter were tackling [nineteenth-century French activist] Frederick Bastiat's writings on socialism's flaws.

Brian C. Anderson, *City Journal*, Summer 2000.

on its telephone survey of 57,278 households. Sarah E. Durkee, legislative assistant for the National Center for Home Education, says that the number of homeschooled children in the United States is approximately 1.9 million. [The writer of this viewpoint], in her book *The Homeschooling Revolution*, estimates that the number was between 893,217 and 990,817 for the 1998-1999 school year. These figures were calculated by contacting state education agencies and, alternatively, homeschool advocacy groups when the state itself did not collect such data.

Legal Questions

Is homeschooling legal?

The National Homeschool Association notes that "homeschooling is legally permitted in all fifty states, but laws and regulations are much more favorable in some states than others." For example, states such as Oklahoma are considered friendly toward homeschooling in that parents are not required to initiate contact with state authorities to begin teaching their children at home. The Commonwealth of Massachusetts, however, is heavily regulated (approval of curriculum, submission of students' work, etc.). Seasoned veterans typically encourage homeschooling parents to become familiar with their state's laws before creating a home-school. This information can be obtained by contacting the head of a local homeschooling support group or state department of education officials.

The favorable legal climate does not mean that skirmishes don't occur. Dean Tong, author of *Elusive Innocence: Survival Guide for the Falsely Accused* (2002) . . . says that a smattering of homeschoolers have had to fight false charges of child abuse. He describes them as the "more impoverished home-schoolers" who are "easier pickings for Child Protection Services." The book taps homeschoolers as a "high-risk" group for being accused of child abuse.

"Based on the phone consultations I've had with (these) homeschoolers, most have been charged in Juvenile-Dependency court with neglect, failure to protect, emotional and psychological abuse, and failure to thrive," reports Tong. Relative to homeschoolers, he says that these unfounded charges are usually made by nosy neighbors who believe children should receive a more formal classroom education. Tong advises parents tossed into this Kafka-like nightmare to immediately "hush-up and retain competent counsel."

Homeschooling Techniques

Are there different methods of homeschooling?

Families may decide to purchase a prepackaged curriculum or textbooks from publishers like A Beka Home School or Saxon Publishers. Others may choose to enroll their children in correspondence programs, like the Calvert School of Maryland, the Christian Liberty Academy of Illinois, or the Clonlara School of Michigan.

Some families opt for a less-structured approach and rely on homemade materials, borrow heavily from local libraries, or craft more innovative projects, like raising rabbits or building homes for the needy, earning Boy Scout merit badges, or taking a cyber class. Tutors may be sought to teach particular skills, such as a foreign language or a musical instrument. Homeschooled children may participate in homeschool learning cooperatives where they can join a choir, take part in a quilting bee, or do a biology lab.

Many home educators increase their learning by attending conferences, subscribing to magazines (like *Homeschooling Today*), or networking through email chains and Internet chat rooms.

Linda Dobson, author of *The First Year of Homeschooling Your Child* (2001), offers this advice about methodology: "Homeschooling gives a family the greatest gift it can receive—time. There's enough time to try many different educational approaches to find the one that best serves your child's needs and learning styles. There is also enough time for your child to play, imagine, dream, and explore."

What about socialization?

This question, as David Boaz of the Cato Institute has observed, is "everybody's favorite" one. Defining socialization is, at best, an arbitrary exercise. Modern schools are filled with students who routinely exhibit cruel, immoral, and, sometimes, criminal behavior. The point of homeschooling may very well be to avoid the company of such miscreants. The burden, however, still seems to fall upon the parents of the homeschooled to make their case. To that end, two studies debunk the myth that homeschoolers are social misfits.

In 1992, Larry Shyers of the University of Florida defended a doctoral dissertation in which he challenged the notion that youngsters at home "lag" in social development. In his study, 8- to 10-year-old children were videotaped at play. Their behavior was observed by trained counselors who did not know which children attended conventional schools and which were homeschooled. The study found no significant difference between the two groups of children in self-concept or assertiveness, which was measured by social development tests. But the videotapes showed that youngsters taught at home by their parents had fewer behavior problems.

Professor A. Bruce Arai, of Wilfrid Laurier University in Canada, wrote a peer-reviewed scholarly analysis titled "Homeschooling and the Redefinition of Citizenship." In his paper, he argues that compulsory schooling cannot be the primary agent for citizenship education. Arai found that homeschooled students "are keen to integrate into the wider society" by noting the high participation levels of homeschoolers in volunteer work and other activities outside the home.

| *"Public schools offer many worthwhile experiences and opportunities not available through home schooling."*

Public Education Is Preferable to Home Schooling

Evie Hudak

Evie Hudak serves on the board of directors of the Colorado Parent-Teachers Association. She is also a member of the Coalition for a Higher Performance Education System and the National Association of State Boards of Education. In the viewpoint that follows, Hudak argues that public schools offer students qualified teachers, high academic standards, safe learning environments, and social interaction—elements that home education may not necessarily provide. Public education is a better choice than home schooling because it provides a wide variety of resources and experiences, including the opportunity for youths to develop the social skills necessary for success in adulthood, Hudak maintains.

As you read, consider the following questions:
1. How are public school teachers held accountable for their work, according to Hudak?
2. What kinds of people comprise Colorado's public school "accountability committees," according to the author?
3. In Hudak's view, what encourages public school students to take more responsibility for their learning?

Public schools are still the best place for children to get an education. They promote student achievement successfully because of the strong system of accountability behind them, which home schools do not have.

Furthermore, public schools offer many worthwhile experiences and opportunities not available through home schooling.

Well-Qualified Teachers

The most important reason public schools provide an excellent education is that teachers are required to be highly qualified. They must acquire and maintain a license to teach. In order to earn this teaching certification, they must demonstrate proficiency in all basic skills, study their subject area in depth, learn effective techniques of instructing all kinds of learners and get on-the-job training under the guidance of an experienced teacher.

To maintain their license, they must continue their own education and training throughout their entire teaching career. Teachers are also held accountable by an ongoing process of evaluation. State laws that provide the requirements for teacher certification and evaluation are regularly reviewed and updated. On the other hand, there are no requirements that parents doing home schooling be trained, experienced, certified or evaluated—or have any particular qualifications.

Standards and Accountability

The accountability in public education is also extensive in the area of academic standards. Public-school students must demonstrate adequate academic achievement.

Colorado public schools have rigorous content standards required for all academic areas, and schools' success in upholding the standards is evaluated by regular statewide and district testing. This process has been strengthened by [a July 1998] law directing the state to base its accreditation of school districts primarily on their performance in the assessment program.

On the other hand, home-schooled students are not required to demonstrate academic achievement on the state assessments, and their curriculum is not compelled to include any standards.

Public education in Colorado is enhanced by another kind of accountability as well, one that calls for involvement of parents and community members in school improvement planning. All schools and school districts in the state are required by law to have a committee of parents, teachers, administrators and community members. These "accountability committees" must evaluate the success of the school or district in providing for student achievement and a safe learning environment, and they advise on strategies for improvement. They are also charged with consulting on the use of taxpayers' money in the budget.

A Taste of Independence

Home educators who claim that their children have plenty of friends and social contacts miss the point. School is a child's first taste of independence, the first chance to discover they are not the centre of the universe and to adapt accordingly. These fundamental friendships and experiences cannot be replicated in the home with the help of a textbook on creative education and a borrowed Bunsen burner.

Our schools may not be perfect but that is partly the point. No child will sail through their education without encountering some problem, whether it be bullying, bad teaching or difficulty in learning. How a child, with the help of supportive parents and school, responds to these problems and overcomes them is as valuable a part of the educational process as learning to read and write.

Gillian Bowditch, *Sunday Times (London)*, January 6, 2002.

The input from the diversity of people making up these committees provides public schools with a kind of broad oversight and opportunity for new ideas not available to home schools.

A Commitment to Basic Values

Besides the kinds of accountability already mentioned, public schools also provide a commitment to building and maintaining the basic values of our society and our democratic system of government. The Colorado Constitution provides for a "thorough and uniform system of free public schools."

The people who govern public schools are elected by the

public and expected to uphold the shared values of the community. School board members receive frequent and regular feedback from the public about their management of the district.

Also, principals, teachers and other school staff receive feedback from parents, parent groups and accountability committees. The public ensures that there is ideological control over public schools.

In home schools, there is no assurance that values such as citizenship and acceptance of diversity will be encouraged. The importance of these values to our nation's survival prompted our founding fathers to support the right to a free education.

Socialization

In addition to instilling values related to citizenship and acceptance of others, public schools boost children's development of social skills and employability skills that are critical to their becoming successful adults.

Because the classes in public schools are large, students are not "spoon-fed." They are forced to take more responsibility for their learning; this helps them gain more independence and initiative, which makes them better employees.

Children in public schools have to deal with many different personalities and temperaments, helping them acquire the skills to interact with the diversity of people in the world at large. They also learn to adapt to the varied leadership styles of teachers. Home-schooled children experience a homogenous group of people, sometimes only their parents.

Public schools help children become more cultured, discriminating and enlightened because they have a wide variety of resources and activities. Schools have music, sports, clubs and other student groups that give children an opportunity to learn more than pure academics and have many kinds of experiences.

Despite the few recent incidents of violence, public schools do provide children with a safe environment in which to learn. In fact, many more incidents of children's gun deaths occur in homes.

Gully Stanford, member of the Colorado Board of Education, explains best why public education surpasses home schooling. "In an increasingly diverse and technological society, the paramount need is to prepare our youth for productive citizenship: No home, no matter how well equipped, can duplicate the nurturing and coping experience of a public school education," he said.

"Single-sex education matters, and it matters most to the students who historically have been denied access to it."

Single-Sex Schools Deserve Support

Karen Stabiner

Single-sex public schools and classes are a viable educational alternative, argues Karen Stabiner in the following viewpoint. Poor, minority, and female students often perform better in single-sex educational environments, where youths often feel less distracted and develop a stronger sense of competency and self-esteem. Girls and boys, moreover, have different learning styles and rates of development and can benefit from teaching methods that are responsive to the way each gender processes information, the author explains. While single-sex education is certainly not a cure-all for the problems faced by public schools, it should be accepted as an educational option. Stabiner is the author of *All Girls: Single-Sex Education and Why It Matters.*

As you read, consider the following questions:
1. According to Stabiner, what kind of students attended single-sex schools in the past? Why?
2. What is the goal of single-sex education, in the author's opinion?
3. What are some of the potential drawbacks to single-sex education, in Stabiner's view?

Karen Stabiner, "Boys Here, Girls There," *Washington Post National Weekly Edition*, vol. 19, May 20–26, 2002, p. 23. Copyright © 2002 by Karen Stabiner. Reproduced by permission.

Many parents may be wondering what the fuss was about [in May 2002] when the Bush administration endorsed single-sex public schools and classes. Separating the sexes was something we did in the days of auto shop and home ec, before Betty Friedan, Gloria Steinem and Title IX.[1] How, then, did an apparent return to the Fifties come to symbolize educational reform?

Here's how: By clearing an alternate, parallel universe where smart matters more than anything, good looks hold little currency and a strong sense of self trumps a date on Saturday night—a place where "class clown" is a label that young boys dread and "math whiz" is a term of endearment for young girls.

I have just spent three years working on a book about two all-girls schools, the private Marlborough School in Los Angeles, and The Young Women's Leadership School of East Harlem (TYWLS), a six-year-old public school in New York City. I went to class, I went home with the girls, I went to dances and basketball games and faculty meetings, and what I learned is this: Single-sex education matters, and it matters most to the students who historically have been denied access to it.

Having said that, I do not intend to proselytize. Single-sex education is not the answer to everyone's prayers. Some children want no part of it and some parents question its relevance. The rest of us should not stop wondering what to do with our coeducational public schools just because of this one new option.

A Valuable Tool

But single-sex education can be a valuable tool—if we target those students who stand to benefit most. For years, in the name of upholding gender equity, we have practiced a kind of harsh economic discrimination. Sociologist Cornelius Riordan says that poor students, minorities and girls stand to profit most from a single-sex environment. Until now,

1. Friedan is the author of the 1963 book *The Feminine Mystique*, considered to be a major influence on the feminist movement. Steinem, feminist author and activist, cofounded *Ms.* magazine. Title IX, part of the Educational Amendments of 1972, prohibits sex discrimination in federally funded educational programs.

though, the only students who could attend a single-sex school were the wealthy ones who could afford private tuition, the relatively few lucky students who received financial aid or those in less-expensive parochial schools. We denied access to the almost 90 percent of American students who attend public schools.

For the fortunate ones—like the girls at Marlborough—the difference is one of attitude, more than any quantifiable measure; their grades and scores may be similar to the graduates of coed prep schools, but they perceive themselves as more competent, more willing to pursue advanced work in fields such as math and science.

At TYWLS, though, the difference is more profound. Students there are predominantly Latina and African American, survivors of a hostile public system. Half of New York's high school students fail to graduate on time, and almost a third never graduate. Throughout the nation, one in six Latina and one in five African American teens become pregnant every year. But most of the members of TYWLS's two graduating classes have gone on to four-year colleges, often the first members of their families to do so, and pregnancy is the stark exception.

There are now 11 single-sex public schools in the United States, all of which serve urban students, many of them in lower-income neighborhoods. Most are side-by-side schools that offer comparable programs for boys and girls in the same facility. The stand-alone girls' schools say that they are compensating for years of gender discrimination; several attempts at similar schools for boys have failed, however, casualties of legal challenges.

Equality Is the Goal

Now, thanks to a bipartisan amendment to President [George W.] Bush's education reform bill, sponsored by Sens. Kay Bailey Hutchison, a Texas Republican, and Hillary Rodham Clinton, a New York Democrat, the administration is about to revise the way it enforces Title IX, to allow for single-sex schools and classes.

The first objection [in May 2002] came from the National Organization for Women [NOW] and the New York Civil

Liberties Union, both of which opposed the opening of TYWLS in the fall of 1996. The two groups continue to insist—as though it were 1896 and they were arguing *Plessy v. Ferguson*[2]—that separate can never be equal. I appreciate NOW's wariness of the Bush administration's endorsement of single-sex public schools, since I am of the generation that still considers the label "feminist" to be a compliment—and many feminists still fear that any public acknowledgment of differences between the sexes will hinder their fight for equality.

Biological Realities

The advocates of single-sex education claim its benefits derive in part from biological realities. Boys' and girls' brains develop differently, they say—differences especially significant for learning in early years. Then, as they get older, boys and girls distract each other from academics because of normal social and sexual development.

"If you put a 15-year-old boy next to a 15-year-old girl, his mind is not going to be on geometry, or Spanish or English," [psychologist Leonard] Sax says. "It's going to be on that girl sexually. He's got the hormones of a grown man, but the brain of a 10-year-old.". . .

Single-sex education helps girls overcome the male sexism that still exists in public schools. "Girls are at center stage with only girls in the audience," says Meg Milne Moulton, co-executive director of the National Coalition of Girls' Schools. "They get 100 percent of the attention."

Kenneth Jost, *CQ Researcher*, July 12, 2002.

But brain research has shown us that girls and boys develop and process information in different ways; they do not even use the same region of the brain to do their math homework. We cannot pretend that such information does not exist just because it conflicts with our ideology. If we hang on to old, quantifiable measurements of equality, we will fail our children. If we take what we learn and use it, we have the chance to do better.

Educators at single-sex schools already get it: Equality is

2. This 1896 Supreme Court decision permitted racial segregation as long as "separate but equal" facilities were available for blacks and whites.

the goal, not the process. There may be more than one path to the destination—but it is the arrival, not the itinerary, that counts.

Coed Is Not Necessarily Better

Some researchers complain that we lack definitive evidence that single-sex education works. There are so many intertwined variables; the students at TYWLS might do well because of smaller class size, passionate teachers and an aggressively supportive atmosphere. Given that, the absence of boys might be beside the point.

The American Association of University Women called for more research even after publishing a 1998 report that showed some girls continued to suffer in the coed classroom. But it is probably impossible to design a study that would retire the question permanently, and, as TYWLS's first principal, Celenia Chevere, liked to say, "What am I supposed to do with these girls in the meantime?"

What is this misplaced reverence for the coed school? Do not think that it was designed with the best interests of all children at heart. As education professors David and Myra Sadker explained in their 1994 book, *Failing at Fairness: How America's Schools Cheat Girls*, our schools were originally created to educate boys. In the late 1700s, girls went to class early in the morning and late in the day—and unlike the boys, they had to pay for the privilege. When families demanded that the public schools do more for their girls, school districts grudgingly allowed the girls into existing classrooms—not because it was the best way to teach children but because no one had the money to build new schools just for girls. Coed classrooms are not necessarily better. They just are.

The Current Challenge

There are 1,200 girls on the waiting list for a handful of spaces in the ninth grade at TYWLS. There is a growing desire for public school alternatives, for an answer more meaningful than a vague if optimistic call for systemwide reform. The demand for single-sex education exists—and now the Bush administration must figure out how to supply it.

Implementation will not be easy. Girls may learn better

without boys, but research and experience show that some boys seem to need the socializing influence of girls: Will there be a group of educational handmaidens, girls who are consigned to coed schools to keep the boys from acting out? Who will select the chosen few who get to go to single-sex schools, and how will they make that choice? Will they take students who already show promise or those who most need help? Or perhaps the philosophy of a new pair of boys' and girls' schools in Albany, N.Y., provides the answer: Take the poorest kids first.

Whatever the approach, no one is calling for a wholesale shift to segregation by gender, and that means someone will be left out. Single-sex public schools perpetuate the kind of two-tiered system that used to be based solely on family income, even if they widen the net. But that has always been true of innovative public schools, and it is no reason to hesitate.

The most troubling question about single-sex public education—Why now?—has nothing to do with school. When support comes so readily from opposite ends of the political spectrum, it is reasonable to ask why everyone is so excited, particularly given the political debate about vouchers and school choice.

If the intention is to strengthen the public school system by responding to new information about how children learn, these classes can serve as a model of innovative techniques, some of which can be transported back into existing coed classrooms. Single-sex public schools and classes, as odd as it may sound, are about inclusion; any school district that wants one can have one and everyone can learn from the experience.

But if this is about siphoning off the best and potentially brightest, and ignoring the rest, then it is a cruel joke, a warm and fuzzy set-up for measures like vouchers. If single-sex becomes a distraction from schools that desperately need help, it serves to further erode the system. The new educational reform law is called the No Child Left Behind Act, an irresistible sentiment with a chilling edge to it—did we ever actually intend to leave certain children behind? The challenge, in developing these new schools and programs, is to make them part of reform, and not an escape hatch from a troubled system.

"A generation of coed schools and dorms and workplaces has produced more equality between men and women, not less."

Single-Sex Schools Do Not Deserve Support

Ellen Goodman

In the following viewpoint syndicated columnist Ellen Goodman maintains that single-sex education is not a beneficial alternative to coeducational public schools. Contrary to the claims of supporters, there is no definitive proof that single-sex schools enhance education for either girls or boys. The promotion of single-sex education is really a step back to the 1950s, when institutionalized sex discrimination limited educational options for girls and boys, Goodman contends. She concludes that youths who learn and live in coeducational environments will be better prepared for a world in which gender equality is increasingly the norm.

As you read, consider the following questions:
1. Who are some of the well-known supporters of single-sex schools, according to the author?
2. What might actually account for the successes of schools like the Young Women's Leadership School of East Harlem, in Goodman's view?
3. In Goodman's opinion, how should educators deal with the problems that boys and girls encounter during adolescence?

Ellen Goodman, "Same-Sex Classes Are a Step Back," *Liberal Opinion Week*, May 27, 2002, p. 11. Copyright © 2002 by Washington Post Writers Group. Reproduced by permission.

With all the talk of "flexibility" you would think the Bush administration was trying to get yoga into the national curriculum instead of single-sex schools.

"Our goal is to provide schools with as much flexibility as possible," said Education Secretary Rod Paige. His announcement encouraging the creation of all-girl and all-boy public schools "flexed" this verbal muscle again and again.

Well, I suppose you have to give them credit for attempting such a pose. What they really want is to revise federal regulations to allow funding for, well, resegregation.

How Did We Get Here?

I'm not surprised that this news came [in early May 2002, when] we found out how badly kids are doing on the national history exam. That's nothing compared to our leaders. They seem to have forgotten that sex segregation was once the baldest of sex discrimination. They've even forgotten the 1950s, when we were educated along separate tracks for separate lives in home ec or shop.

Now the old thing is being touted as the new thing. The restoration is being offered as the reform. Backsliding is being described as "innovation." That's a twist that would challenge a master yogi.

How did we get here? A generation ago, in court and Congress, we agreed that separate was not equal in public schools, whether we were talking about race or gender. The road to equality was walked together.

Now an odd coalition of feminists and conservatives has become "flexible" on civil rights. It includes politicians from Sen. Hillary Clinton, who went to all-girls Wellesley College, to Sen. Kay Bailey Hutchison, who went to the coed University of Texas.

Some supporters of single-sex schools think times have changed so much that women don't have to worry about discrimination. Others believe that the best way for women to break barriers is to take their own road. And still others believe that schools are so bad we shouldn't worry about equal education; we should worry about *any* education.

In this atmosphere, it has become common wisdom to say that girls and boys, especially adolescents, distract and derail each other from the (school) subjects at hand. It has become equally common wisdom to say that girls and boys are different biological creatures who learn at different paces in different ways and therefore do best in different schools.

Most of this wisdom is presented under the rubric: "studies show." But in fact, there is much anecdote and little research to prove that single-sex education benefits either boys *or* girls.

No one knows whether girls do well in schools like the Young Women's Leadership School of East Harlem because of the absence of boys or the presence of small classes and a committed community. No one knows, for that matter, whether boys are distracted by girls or "civilized" by them. Or neither.

A Healthier Preparation

In the civilized world, men and women constantly interact in each other's presence in the workplace and in society. They compete for jobs, for salaries, for cultural attention, for family influence. . . .

A shared educational experience is healthier preparation for the real adult world than a system in which girls and boys grow up knowing nothing about each other's minds. Girls and boys are assumed to think differently. The sooner kids are acquainted with that reality, the better.

Marianne Means, *Liberal Opinion Week*, May 27, 2002.

And while some all-girls schools describe themselves as progressive hothouses of feminism, some all-boys schools— remember the Virginia Military Institute?—tend to act like the last bastions of the tradition.

Can you have separate but equal schools? Is it just a matter of being "flexible" on civil rights?

Title IX, now [more than] 30 years old, allows federal funding of some separate classes like Phys Ed and Sex Ed. But it's quite a different matter to encourage the public funding of schools for only one gender. Can we imagine paying for separate but equal schools to accommodate the "learning styles" or psychic "needs" of separate races? Can we imagine calling for such "flexibility" in civil rights?

Living in a Coed World

We live in a coed world, we work in it. A generation of coed schools and dorms and workplaces has produced more equality between men and women, not less. We are less likely to see each other as "other," less likely to separate our work and personal lives.

Even if, as some worry, girls slip and boys behave badly during adolescence, the solution is not to send them to his and hers corners. It's to experiment with new methods of teaching, and to rewire the small society called school. This school world is, after all, a mirror image of the larger world. Out here, men and women still have one foot in a new world and one in the old. It's a tough pose to hold.

In the climate of despair over public schools, we've been latching onto one "solution" after another. One day it's school uniforms, the next day it's school choice. Now we're saying that a solution to bad public education is single-sex public education.

There are fewer than a dozen single-sex public schools. They will remain a minority. The promise of funding and the premise of "flexibility" is another in a series of deliberate distractions.

Coeducation is not the problem. Education is. And no matter how limber the political stance, you can't keep moving forward while you're looking backward.

Periodical Bibliography

The following articles have been selected to supplement the diverse views presented in this chapter.

Church & State	"Voters and Vouchers: The People Speak," January 2001.
Rachel S. Cox	"Home Schooling Debate," *CQ Researcher*, January 17, 2003.
Facts On File News Services	"Single-Sex Education," *Issues and Controversies On File*, June 7, 2002.
Howard Fuller	"Full Court Press: Why I Am Fighting for School Choice," *Education Next*, Fall 2002.
Jane Gross	"Unhappy in Class, More Are Learning at Home," *New York Times*, November 10, 2003.
Jean C. Halle	"Home Schooling: Why We Should Care," *Education Week*, November 13, 2002.
Jennifer G. Hickey	"Readin', Writin', and Race," *Insight on the News*, January 7, 2003.
John J. Miller	"School Choice, Not an Echo: After the Supreme Court's Decision, the Future of the Movement," *National Review*, July 29, 2002.
Robert E. Pierre	"In Detroit, Skepticism on School Vouchers," *Washington Post*, July 28, 2002.
William Raspberry	"Same-Sex Schools Work—Sometimes," *Washington Post*, March 16, 1998.
Jim Rice	"'School Choice' Passes a Test: A Victory for Vouchers—but Who Wins?" *Sojourners*, September/October 2002.
Massie Ritsch	"Single-Gender Schools Gaining Favor, Success," *Los Angeles Times*, May 28, 2002.
Lawrence Rudden	"Separate and Unequal, Still," *World & I*, March 2002.
Patrick Welsh	"Single-Sex Schools Unbalance Education," *USA Today*, May 15, 2002.
Randall A. Zitterkopf	"Home Schooling: Just Another Silver Bullet," *School Administrator*, December 2000.

CHAPTER 3

What Role Should Religious and Moral Values Play in Public Education?

Chapter Preface

When Greg Valde, a teacher living in Whitewater, Wisconsin, contemplates his young daughter's entrance into public school, he thinks of goals that many people may feel are beyond the pale of government-sponsored education: "I want her to learn and grow in a caring community that challenges her to value honesty over achievement, kindness over popularity, and inspires in her a sense of wonder, connection, and creativity. . . . I do not want her to spend her days in a place where love is rarely mentioned and achievement is an end in itself." Valde regretfully recalls his own past experiences in educational institutions where he learned to place "achievement over celebration, intelligence over morality, and wealth over compassion," and he believes his daughter deserves better.

Valde and other parents concerned about the potentially alienating effects of public schools are finding increasing support from the field of character education. Since the early 1990s, the character education movement—which aims to integrate the teaching of morals and values into public school curricula—has gained strength. For example, a national coalition known as Character Education Partnership (CEP), initially formed in 1993, currently advocates public school agendas that emphasize values. CEP hopes to instill in students "good character," which they define as understanding and acting on core values such as honesty, fairness, respect, caring, effort, and responsibility. To date, thousands of school districts have adopted some form of character education. Some programs incorporate intensive history courses and discussions on controversial topics to foster democratic ideals and moral understanding. Other programs encourage moral reflection across the curriculum, with teachers introducing core values through the study of science, literature, and social studies. Still others focus on inspiring a sense of responsibility and community through school assemblies, homeroom discussions, and volunteer activities.

Character education itself is not new. In the 1830s many schools used the *McGuffey Reader*, a book that combined biblical messages with poems, stories, and catchphrases to teach students about important values. But many of today's character education programs eschew a biblical emphasis and concentrate instead on teaching "universal" values that transcend religious and cultural differences. Herein lies their weakness, critics contend. Columnist Don Feder, for example, maintains that public-school character education will inevitably fail because of its attempt to teach morality without mentioning religion. "Caring, honesty, responsibility and respect for others are universal because they were ordained by the Master of the Universe," states Feder. He believes that without an expressed faith in God, the lessons of character educators will ring hollow. For this reason, Feder concludes, "Ethics is best left to families, religious institutions and private schools. Public education will only muck things up."

Whether public schools can and should teach ethical values is one of the subjects debated by the authors in the following chapter. Two other hotly contested issues involving values and education—the proposal to display the Ten Commandments in public schools and the teaching of evolution versus the teaching of creationism—are also discussed.

> *"A school committed to character strives to become a microcosm of a civil, caring, and just society."*

Schools Should Provide Character Education

Tom Lickona, Eric Schaps, and Catherine Lewis

Character education promotes the teaching of ethical values and moral behavior in primary and secondary schools. In the following viewpoint Tom Lickona, Eric Schaps, and Catherine Lewis maintain that character education fosters universally accepted virtues such as honesty, caring, and fairness. They argue that schools should adopt a comprehensive approach to character development in which the teaching process, the curriculum, sports and club activities, and staff behavior all reflect basic ethical principles. Lickona heads the Center for the Fourth and Fifth R's at the State University of New York at Cortland. Schaps is president of the Developmental Studies Center in Oakland, California. Lewis is a senior research scientist at Mills College in Oakland, California.

As you read, consider the following questions:
1. What is the "hidden curriculum," according to the authors?
2. In the authors' view, in what way might students practice the skills that character education intends to promote?
3. How should school staff "take ownership" of the character education effort, in the authors' opinion?

C haracter education holds that widely shared, pivotally important, core ethical values—such as caring, honesty, fairness, responsibility, and respect for self and others—form the basis of good character. A school committed to character development stands for these values (sometimes referred to as "virtues" or "character traits"), defines them in terms of behaviors that can be observed in the life of the school, models these values, studies and discusses them, uses them as the basis of human relations in the school, celebrates their manifestations in the school and community, and holds all school members accountable to standards of conduct consistent with the core values.

In a school committed to developing character, these core values are treated as a matter of obligation, as having a claim on the conscience of the individual and community. Character education asserts that the validity of these values, and our responsibility to uphold them, derive from the fact that such values affirm our human dignity, promote the development and welfare of the individual person, serve the common good, meet the classical tests of reversibility (i.e., Would you want to be treated this way?) and universality (i.e., Would you want all persons to act this way in a similar situation?), and inform our rights and responsibilities in a democratic society. The school makes clear that these basic human values transcend religious and cultural differences, and express our common humanity.

A Comprehensive Approach

Good character involves understanding, caring about, and acting upon core ethical values. A holistic approach to character development therefore seeks to develop the cognitive, emotional, and behavioral aspects of moral life. Students grow to understand core values by studying and discussing them, observing behavioral models, and resolving problems involving the values. Students learn to care about core values by developing empathy skills, forming caring relationships, helping to create community, hearing illustrative and inspirational stories, and reflecting on life experiences. And they learn to act upon core values by developing prosocial behaviors (e.g., communicating feelings, active listening, helping skills) and by repeatedly practicing these behaviors, especially in the context of relationships (e.g., through cross-age tutoring, mediating conflicts, community service). As children grow in character, they develop an increasingly refined understanding of the core values, a deeper commitment to living according to those values, and a stronger capacity and tendency to behave in accordance with them.

Schools committed to character development look at themselves through a moral lens to assess how virtually everything that goes on in school affects the character of students. A comprehensive approach uses all aspects of schooling as opportunities for character development. This includes what is sometimes called *the hidden curriculum* (e.g., school ceremonies and procedures; the teachers' example; students' relationships with teachers, other school staff, and each other; the instructional process; how student diversity is addressed; the assessment of learning; the management of the school environment; the discipline policy); the *academic curriculum* (i.e., core subjects, including the health curriculum); and *extracurricular programs* (i.e., sports teams, clubs, service projects, after-school care). "Stand alone" character education programs can be useful first steps or helpful elements of an ongoing effort but are not an adequate substitute for a holistic approach that integrates character development into every aspect of school life. Finally, rather than simply waiting for opportunities to arise, with an intentional and proactive approach, the school staff takes deliberate steps for developing character, drawing wherever possible on practices shown by research to be effective.

A school committed to character strives to become a microcosm of a civil, caring, and just society. It does this by creating a community that helps all its members form caring attachments to one another. This involves developing caring relationships among students (within and across grade levels), among staff, between students and staff, and between staff and families. These caring relationships foster both the desire to learn and the desire to be a good person. All children and adolescents have needs for safety, belonging, and the experience of contributing, and they are more likely to internalize the values and expectations of groups that meet these needs.

Likewise, if staff members and parents experience mutual respect, fairness, and cooperation in their relationships with each other, they are more likely to develop the capacity to promote those values in students. In a caring school community, the daily life of classrooms and all other parts of the school environment (e.g., the corridors, cafeteria, playground, school bus, front office, and teachers' lounge) are imbued with a climate of concern and respect for others.

Opportunities for Moral Action

In the ethical as in the intellectual domain, students are constructive learners; they learn best by doing. To develop good character, they need many and varied opportunities to apply values such as compassion, responsibility, and fairness in everyday interactions and discussions as well as through community service. By grappling with real-life challenges (e.g., how to divide the labor in a cooperative learning group, how to reach consensus in a class meeting, how to reduce fights on the playground, how to carry out a service learning project) and reflecting on these experiences, students develop practical understanding of the requirements of cooperating with others and giving of oneself. Through repeated moral experiences, students develop and practice the skills and behavioral habits that make up the action side of character.

A Meaningful Curriculum

When students succeed at the work of school and feel a sense of competence and autonomy, they are more likely to feel valued and cared about as persons. Because students come to school with diverse skills, interests and needs, an academic program that helps all students succeed will be one in which the content and pedagogy are sophisticated enough to engage all learners. This means providing a curriculum that is inherently interesting and meaningful to students. A meaningful curriculum includes active teaching and learning methods such as cooperative learning, problem-solving approaches, and experience-based projects. These approaches increase student autonomy by appealing to students' interests, providing them with opportunities to think creatively and test their ideas, and fostering a sense of "voice and choice"—having a say in decisions and plans that affect them.

In addition, effective character educators look for the natural intersections between the academic content they wish to teach and the character qualities they wish to develop. These "character connections" can take many forms, such as addressing current ethical issues in science, debating historical practices and decisions, and discussing character traits and ethical dilemmas in literature. When teachers bring to the fore the character dimension of the curriculum, they enhance the relevance of subject matter to students' natural interests and questions, and in the process, increase student engagement and achievement.

Fostering Self-Motivation

Character is often defined as "doing the right thing when no one is looking." The best underlying ethical reason for following rules, for example, is respect for the rights and needs of others—not fear of punishment or desire for a reward. Similarly, we want students to be kind to others because of an inner belief that kindness is good and a desire to be a kind person. Growing in self-motivation is a developmental process that schools of character are careful not to undermine by excessive emphasis on extrinsic incentives. When such schools give appropriate social recognition for students' prosocial actions (e.g., "Thank you for holding the door—that was a thoughtful thing to do.") or celebrate character through special awards (e.g., for outstanding school or community service), they keep the focus on character. Schools of character work with students to develop their understanding of rules, their awareness of how their behavior affects others, and the character strengths—such as self-control, perspective taking, and conflict resolution skills— needed to act responsibly in the future. Rather than settle for mere compliance, these schools seek to help students benefit from their mistakes by providing meaningful opportunities for reflection, problem solving, and restitution.

Adults Should Model Core Values

All school staff—teachers, administrators, counselors, school psychologists, coaches, secretaries, cafeteria workers, playground aides, bus drivers—need to be involved in learning about, discussing, and taking ownership of the character education effort. First and foremost, staff members assume this responsibility by modeling the core values in their own behavior and taking advantage of other opportunities to influence the students with whom they interact.

Character and Achievement

Of course I want my daughter to learn to read and write and calculate and understand history and science, but only in a context that honors effort, kindness, integrity, laughter, and balance. I do not want her to spend her days in a place where love is rarely mentioned and achievement is an end in and of itself. I want her to learn to write because she finds in it a way to connect to others and explore her self. I want her to read difficult things because she seeks to understand and believes in facing and meeting challenges. And I want her to study government because she feels a sense of responsibility to build a better society. That is, I want her achievement in school to follow from her spirit and character. I do not think it works the other way around.

Gregory A. Valde, *Tikkun*, September 1999.

Second, the same values and norms that govern the life of students serve to govern the collective life of adult members in the school community. Like students, adults grow in character by working collaboratively with each other and participating in decision-making that improves classrooms and school. They also benefit from extended staff development and opportunities to observe colleagues and then apply character development strategies in their own work with students.

Third, a school that devotes time to staff reflection on moral matters helps to ensure that it operates with integrity. Through faculty meetings and smaller support groups, a reflective staff regularly asks questions such as: What character-building experiences is the school already providing for its students? What negative moral experiences (e.g., peer cruelty, student cheating, adult disrespect of students, littering of the grounds) is the school currently failing to address? And what important moral experiences (e.g., cooperative learning, school and community service, opportunities to learn about and interact with people from different racial, ethnic, and socioeconomic backgrounds) is the school now omitting? What school practices are at odds with its professed core values and desire to develop a caring school community? Reflection of this nature is an indispensable condition for developing the moral life of a school.

Schools that are engaged in effective character education have leaders (e.g., the principal, a lead teacher or counselor, a district administrator, or preferably a small group of such individuals) who champion the effort. At least initially, many schools and districts establish a character education committee—often composed of staff, students, parents, and possibly community members—that takes responsibility for planning, implementation, and support. Over time, the regular governing bodies of the school or district may take on the functions of this committee. The leadership also takes steps to provide for the long-range support (e.g., adequate staff development, time to plan) of the character education initiative, including, ideally, support at the district and state levels. In addition, within the school students assume developmentally appropriate roles in leading the character education effort through class meetings, student government, peer mediation, cross-age tutoring, service clubs, task forces, and student-led initiatives.

Involving Families

Schools that reach out to families and include them in character-building efforts greatly enhance their chances for success with students. They take pains at every stage to communicate with families—via newsletters, e-mails, family nights, and parent conferences—about goals and activities regarding character education. To build greater trust between home and school, parents are represented on the character education committee. These schools also make a special effort to reach out to subgroups of parents who may not feel part of the school community. Finally, schools and families enhance the effectiveness of their partnership by recruiting the help of the wider community (i.e., businesses, youth organizations, religious institutions, the government, and the media) in promoting character development.

"It is doubtful that school programs will prove successful if they seek to teach children the lessons that adults have not yet learned."

Character Education Will Likely Fail

Thomas J. Lasley II

Character education—a program for fostering moral values and behavior in elementary and high school students—is not likely to succeed, argues Thomas J. Lasley II in the following viewpoint. Those who implement character education mean well, but the values taught in schools often conflict with the values espoused in the mass media, Lasley explains. Furthermore, the behavior of teachers and parents often reinforces competitiveness and individualism—negating the cooperation and altruism that character education intends to promote. The best way to teach values is for adults to become people of integrity themselves, the author concludes. Lasley is a professor in the School of Education at the University of Dayton in Ohio.

As you read, consider the following questions:

1. In what way is character education similar to sex education and drug education, according to Lasley?
2. According to John Condry, cited by the author, how many acts of violence occur in every hour of children's television programming?
3. How do teachers undermine character education, in Lasley's opinion?

Thomas J. Lasley II, "The Missing Ingredient of Character Education," *Phi Delta Kappan*, vol. 78, April 1997, p. 654. Copyright © 1997 by Phi Delta Kappa, Inc. Reproduced by permission of the publisher and the author.

Educators in the U.S. are embracing another "new" panacea for the apparent crisis of values in the schools. This time it's "character education." Teachers, administrators, and even parents resonate to the idea of teaching students the core values deemed essential for cultural survival. Some states (e.g., Maryland) have devised ways of instilling specific "pro-social values" into young people as prerequisites for graduation. Some school districts—from Los Angeles (the Thomas Jefferson Center) to Dayton (the Allen School) to Bath, Maine (Character First)—have implemented specific programs to create values-enriched educational experiences.

Cultural Values Versus School Values

The values juggernaut looks good on the surface. The Jefferson Center reports a sharp drop in discipline problems and enhanced student responsibility. The Allen School and other values-oriented programs offer similar testimonials and data that confirm their success.

Americans want the school to accomplish what is not occurring in the home. All too often social problems that seem beyond the reach of the living room are foisted off on the classroom. In this respect, character education is akin to such initiatives as sex education or drug education. But it is similar in another way as well: all three connect what children see with what they are told. The medium becomes entangled with the message. Children learn just as much, if not more, from what they see as from what they hear. Sex, drug, and character education can be built around a curriculum (a variety of books and manuals), but they are made real by what students see in the behaviors of those who communicate the message.

Whether adults like it or not, values are learned through observation and, as Aristotle noted, through practice. Social learning complicates efforts to teach values. Communities are now more pluralistic than ever, and the curriculum that students experience is filled with messages from the culture that frequently conflict with the values that schools teach. Character education programs espouse responsibility, while the culture sends a strong countervailing message: "If it feels good, do it!"

Emphasizing the Worst

The dissonance, though, is not just embedded in the messages of the media. It is also apparent in the daily communication that occurs between children and adults both in the home and at school. The reason the character education movement will lose its luster is not because it is fundamentally wrong, but because adults are fundamentally flawed and seemingly proud of it. American culture, at least as presented in the media, tends to emphasize the worst, not the best, in human beings. What children see on television, according to John Condry, a professor of human development and family studies at Cornell University, are innumerable nihilistic messages that include an average of 25 acts of violence every hour (and this during the children's programs) and six pro-drug advertisements for every anti-drug message. Indeed, writes Condry, "Commercials designed especially for children had lower frequencies than the overall sample for nearly all so-called altruistic values. . . . Commercials on programs designed for children rarely stressed being helpful or obedient. . . . The values stressed by commercials . . . [extolled] selfish and self-serving values over altruistic values."

Kelley. © 1998 by *San Diego Union-Tribune*, Copley News Service. Reproduced by permission.

Television is not the most dangerous culprit, though. When children are not at home watching television, they are at school observing teachers—and learning values. School environments, though changing in some positive ways, still represent hostile territory for many young people. Teachers tell students to cooperate, but then they systematically rank students in terms of their class performance. As a consequence, children quickly learn that in school one has to do more than simply read; one must read better than one's neighbor. Teachers tell students that respect is essential for social responsibility, but then they call on boys a majority of the time when conducting classroom discussions. And, finally, students are informed that they should be critical thinkers, but then they are evaluated on whether they think the same way that their teachers do. Students who do think critically are often labeled as difficult or obstreperous.

Values are caught, not taught. And once caught, they must be practiced. No short cuts to virtue exist. If the media messages and school policies make values difficult to catch, parental behavior and personal self-absorption (i.e., American individualism) exacerbate the social learning experience. Parents are busy. When they are not working, they are getting ready for work. And when they are not "readying" themselves, they are trying to cope with personal frustrations that can overwhelm them. The emphasis on doing what is right for me is the rule, even if the consequences for children are pernicious. The primacy of the individual in American culture short-circuits the capacity of many Americans to see beyond themselves. And this myopia threatens efforts to communicate meaningful prosocial values in the schools.

According to many experts, the need for character education is a result of the value neutral stance of schools during the 1960s and 1970s. The antidote for value neutrality, they claim, is value advocacy. Those same advocates now prescriptively know which values are "right" and socially beneficial: compassion, responsibility, courage, and perseverance.

But advocacy is easy. The real challenge is changing the behavior of all those who influence children. Unfortunately, our character flaws make it easier to undermine the value dispositions of young people than to teach them. The answer is not adult perfection. Our goal should be to become people of good character. That goal is achievable if we adults can see people as ends, not means; if we can see that people matter and need to be taken seriously and respected; and if we can see that we must be responsible as individuals for our own behavior. In a culture in which more people claim victim status and fewer people think beyond their individual needs, it is doubtful that school programs will prove successful if they seek to teach children the lessons that adults have not yet learned.

"The first small step in creating a healthier moral climate can start [with posting the Ten Commandments in schools]."

The Ten Commandments Should Be Posted in Public Schools

Dennis Teti

Congress should permit the Ten Commandments to be displayed in public schools, argues Dennis Teti in the following viewpoint. The misguided ban on any recognition of religion in public schools has resulted in an immoral environment that breeds student violence, Teti maintains. Allowing the Ten Commandments to be posted in schools could provoke a timely discussion between teachers and students on the value of self-discipline and moral rules, he concludes. Teti is an associate professor of government at Regent University's Northern Virginia/District of Columbia Graduate Center.

As you read, consider the following questions:
1. What is the Ten Commandments Defense Act, according to Teti?
2. In the author's opinion, what is hidden beneath the seemingly "neutral" stance regarding religious belief and nonbelief?
3. What was George Washington's position on religion and education, according to Teti?

Violence in our nation's schools has been growing since the Columbine High School killings [in April 1999]. The [March 2001] shooting at Santana High School in Santee, California, has been followed by copycat acts and threats of violence around the country.

In 1999 the House of Representatives, revulsed by Columbine, amended its juvenile justice reform bill to include the Ten Commandments Defense Act (TCDA). 45 Democrats joined 203 Republicans to support TCDA, but the measure disappeared in the swamp of Senate politics.

The Ten Commandments Defense Act

Since the . . . violence . . . in Santee, Congress doesn't know what to do. Here's a suggestion: Revive and enact the Ten Commandments Defense Act. Now it will have the support of a president who has said that students must learn the difference between right and wrong.

TCDA is a simple bill designed to protect federalism against judicial encroachment. First, it would recognize the powers of states and localities to display the Ten Commandments in schools and other government owned buildings. Second, it would recognize the right of individuals to practice their religious faith by prayer or other expression on government owned property so long as the rights of others are not interfered with. Third, it would instruct federal statutory courts to decide cases according to this law.

TCDA was originally aimed at a rather silly 1980 Supreme Court ruling that overturned a Kentucky requirement posting the Decalogue in public schools. The unconstitutional defect of these displays, said the 5 to 4 majority, was that they might "induce the schoolchildren to read, meditate upon, perhaps to venerate and obey, the Commandments." This is "not a permissible state objective."

The measure was also intended to forestall a new decision striking down student-led prayer at sports events, a holding which was actually handed down [in June 2000] by a 6 to 3 majority, in *Santa Fe Independent School District v. Roe*.

Opponents ridicule the notion that there is any connection between school violence and bans on official Ten Commandments displays. Indeed it would be silly to pretend that teenagers don't know murder is a crime merely because they are not allowed to see the Commandment "thou shalt not kill."

Teenagers who harm others are old enough to bear responsibility for their own acts. Yet the same liberals who deny any impact which firm moral instructions might have on the young seem to blame everything else in youth culture for students who run amok. The Columbine killers, who didn't share the school's sports enthusiasms, were called "freaks"; the alleged Santee High School shooter was small and called "scrawny." What is the common theme here? Victimization and lack of self-esteem—the liberal claim that the social environment makes killers out of young people who don't "fit in."

The one change in school culture that would focus attention on the wrong of violence—fostering the Ten Commandments—is vociferously opposed by liberals. Still, is there no connection between judicial decisions driving religion out of schools and student violence entering them?

The Foundation of Religious Freedom

Until 1947 the policy laid down by the American Founders was usually followed, according to which government should support religious belief on a nonpreferential basis. The Founders' most official statement of their policy is contained in the Northwest Ordinance of 1787, drafted by a committee including Thomas Jefferson. Under the ordinance, which is one of our nation's organic laws, the federal government ruled the Northwest Territories until they became states. Article III declares that education and religion are intertwined: "Religion, morality, and knowledge being necessary to good government and the happiness of mankind, schools and the means of education shall forever be encouraged." To this day many state constitutions include similar language. The Founders saw no conflict in Article I: "No person, demeaning himself in a peaceable and orderly manner, shall ever be molested on account of his mode of worship, or religious sentiments. . . ." The law meant that religious faith is the buttress of religious freedom.

Of course in practice the policy of nonpreferential support has not always been easy to carry out, but communities across the country have generally found ways of accommodating differing religious demands. It's not too much to say that, far from creating religious conflict, the very need for balancing differences in each community was among the most invaluable civic benefits of the Founders' policy. The process of accommodation forces diverse religious traditions to learn more about each other and to become tolerant without sacrificing religious and moral commitment.

A Radical Departure

In 1947 the Supreme Court radically departed from the Founders' religious policy by erecting a so-called "wall of separation" between religion and public order. In *Everson v. Board of Education*, the Court pronounced—falsely—that according to the Founders, government was supposed to be "neutral" not only among groups of religious believers but between religious groups and groups of "non-believers"—in short, between religion and non-religion. In [Abraham] Lincoln's words, this is like trying to find some *tertium quid*[1] between a living and a dead man. And even as Lincoln showed that in practice the idea of official neutrality between pro-slavery and anti-slavery views hid a "covert zeal for slavery," the liberal position of official "neutrality" regarding religious belief and nonbelief conceals a covert zeal *for* irreligion.

For Morality's Sake

For those who support posting the Ten Commandments in schools the issue is simple. Morals are declining and the Ten Commandments teach morals. Therefore, they contend, posting the Ten Commandments in schools will boost the moral character of America's schoolchildren. The result, they say, will be less violence and a higher general level of morality in the U.S. "By . . . posting the Ten Commandments, we help kids be better citizens and we make school a safer place," says Colorado state Sen. John Andrews (R).

Facts On File News Service, *Issues and Controversies On File*, March 15, 2002.

There is no other way to explain why the Supreme Court—led by the ACLU [American Civil Liberties Union] and other lawyer interest groups—has systematically driven

---

1. a "third something" produced by the union of two opposing things

every recognition of religion out of government schools, from classroom prayer and Bible-reading exercises to clergy-led invocations at graduations and any other display that libertarian lawyers might interpret as favoring belief in God. One federal judge has ordered monitors to patrol Alabama school halls to snitch on anyone found praying in the unhallowed precincts.

George Washington's Farewell Address represented the general opinion on morality and religion of the same Founders who wrote religious liberty into the First Amendment. Political prosperity, by which he meant the safety and happiness of the people, cannot be obtained by those who won't obey the rules of morality. "Where is the security for property, for reputation, for life, if the sense of religious obligation *desert* the oaths, which are the instruments of investigation in Courts of Justice?" he asked. Inculcating morals ("values clarification" in current jargon) without religion is useless:

"Whatever may be conceded to the influence of refined education on minds of peculiar structure, reason and experience both forbid us to expect that National morality can prevail in exclusion of religious principle." For the Founders and the Constitution of freedom they gave us, the equation is simple: no security without morality; no morality without religion. Over more than a century and a half when that equation governed, students killing students at random was unimaginable. Student crime rarely went beyond sneaking smokes in the school bathroom.

Simple Solutions

Ronald Reagan used to make liberals roll their eyes by saying that the answers to some social problems are simple. Teen emotions run high, as every parent knows. The young need as much assistance as society can give them, individually and communally, in order to learn and practice self-discipline. When schools scowl at religion by excluding it from official acknowledgment, they also frown on morality. However unintentionally, they teach students that moral behavior is a "choice," a subjective or private issue unlike, for instance, modern biology, the knowledge of which is objectively true and can't rationally be disbelieved.

The claim is simply not credible that to teach students that murder violates "the laws of nature and of nature's God" establishes a state religion. It's far more credible to expect some troubled teenagers, barred from learning that God and reason forbid killing, to contemplate and carry out murder.

How can posting the Ten Commandments in schools begin to restore a culture in which the basic moral injunctions on which our liberty and safety are premised are given official notice? Displaying the Tables of the Law does nothing in itself, but it can stimulate a much needed discussion among inquisitive students, teachers, and officials: Why these rules? What is their source? Why must they be followed? Don't they conflict with my freedom? The first small step in creating a healthier moral climate can start here. The Ten Commandments Defense Act doesn't require states and communities to display them, but the Act would allow and encourage them to do so without judicial interference. Congress should enact it before more Columbines and Santanas raise the teen death toll.

"Pushing the Ten Commandments as a moral code is bad ethics, bad religion, and bad psychology."

The Ten Commandments Should Not Be Posted in Public Schools

Lewis Vaughn

In the viewpoint that follows, Lewis Vaughn denounces recent proposals to post the Ten Commandments in public schools. In his opinion the Ten Commandments are a list of vague, simplistic rules that lack genuine moral authority because they do not address the complexities of modern life. Furthermore, there is no evidence that prayer, Bible reading, and other religious practices and codes make public schools safer, as some have claimed. Children should learn that morality is rooted in empathy and a clear understanding of the issue in question—not in absolutism and dogma, writes Vaughn. Vaughn is the editor of *Free Inquiry*, a journal published by the Council for Secular Humanism.

As you read, consider the following questions:
1. In what ways do the Ten Commandments conflict with each other, according to Vaughn?
2. In the author's view, why are absolutist codes immoral?
3. How could posting the Ten Commandments in schools actually cause conflict, in Vaughn's opinion?

What can shield my teenage children against school violence better than metal detectors and security guards? Some parents say there's something as good as a flak jacket: Posting the Ten Commandments on the wall. Since the Columbine High massacre in Colorado [in 1999], plenty of clergy, politicians, and elected officials have insisted that the Ten Commandments be displayed in schools, in government buildings, and in courtrooms. The postings, they say, will curb violence and save society. Opponents of the idea scream "church-state separation" and label it bad government. But it's more than just bad government—it's bad for my children. It's bad for them because pushing the Ten Commandments as a moral code is bad ethics, bad religion, and bad psychology. Here's why:

Conflicting and Vague

1. They conflict with one another. We're commanded not to kill and not to lie. But what if the only way to prevent the killing of a person is to tell a lie? Or to steal? The Commandments by themselves offer no help in resolving such conflicts. To resolve them, you must appeal to moral principles that are outside the scope of the Commandments.

2. They are too vague to be useful. We're commanded to "honor thy father and thy mother." Does this apply even when the father abuses his children or batters his wife? It's not clear. We're commanded not to kill. Does this mean we cannot kill in self-defense? That we cannot kill to save lives? The 10 C's are fuzzy. And to unfuzz them you have to interpret them by appealing to a moral theory.

3. They are inadequate. Can the Ten Commandments guide us in making the toughest moral choices of our lives? Can they tell us what our moral duties are regarding capital punishment, racism, gay rights, women's rights, overpopulation, artificial insemination, and the rationing of health care? The 10 C's moral code is no more enlightening in such cases than a restaurant menu.

An Immoral Menu

4. They are absolutist to the point of being immoral. Like some secular systems of ethics (Immanuel Kant's, for example), the

Ten Commandments admit no exceptions. Thou shall not—regardless. If a man has starving children and the only way to feed them is to steal food, he must not steal, even if his children die. A code that sanctions such acts is immoral. Those who try to stick to absolutist codes are like moronic hikers who walk off a cliff because they were told to stay the course.

Ramsey. © 2000 by Copley News Service. Reproduced by permission.

5. They have no divine authority. The Ten Commandments are presumed to have divine authority. To many, this means that certain acts are right or wrong because God says they're right or wrong. That is, God is the author of morality; there is no morality independent of God's commandments. If God had not said that adultery was wrong, it would not be wrong. But if this were true, then God could just as easily have commanded that we go forth and murder our mothers, rape our neighbors, and rob our friends. And God's saying that these actions are right would make them right. But this is absurd. Clearly these actions would be wrong regardless of what God commanded.

6. There is no evidence that they work. Posting the Ten Commandments is supposed to change people's behavior. Teens will stop shooting teens. Drug abuse will wane. This is an empirical claim that can be tested scientifically. Trouble is, there is no evidence at all for this claim. Commandment supporters say that, when prayer and Bible-reading were in the schools, morality was higher and crime was lower. Critics reply that, when God was in the schools, racism and gang wars were up and tolerance for religious minorities was down. Fact is, such correlations are not well established, if at all. And even if they were, correlations are not the same thing as cause and effect. If they were, we could plausibly claim that religion causes school shootings since most of the recent high-profile school shootings involved assailants who were religious.

Worse still, posting the Ten Commandments in school is likely to *cause* conflict because they are partisan. There are several versions—Protestant, Catholic, and others—each based on a different dogma. There is no "standard" version, as George W. Bush recently suggested. Whose version should get posted? Fight! Fight!

Sending the Wrong Message

7. *They give children the wrong message about morality.* I want my teenage children to understand that there's more to being moral than trying to adhere to simplistic rules. Life is more complicated than that and so is morality. I want them to see that there is such a thing as objective morality—but that morality can't be put on a bumper sticker. I want them to learn how to work from an overriding moral theory that makes sense of moral principles and helps resolve conflicts among them. I want them to be mature enough to reject ethics that fly in the face of our considered moral judgments. I want them to do the right thing because they have empathy and understanding of what's at stake—not because dogma compels them. And I want them to make good choices and take responsibility for every one of them.

My children are not in daycare, and I don't want them using a daycare version of ethics.

"Science teachers should not advocate any religious interpretations of nature and should be nonjudgmental about the personal beliefs of students."

Creationism Should Be Excluded from Science Courses

National Science Teachers Association

In the viewpoint that follows, the National Science Teachers Association (NSTA) contends that creationism—a nonscientific and religious view of biological origins—should not be included in science curricula. Evolutionary theory, which asserts that life developed through a process of mutation and natural selection, is based on scientific observation and evidence, the authors point out. It is the unifying concept of science that all students should learn. Administrators and teachers should not give in to pressure from sectarian groups to downplay the significance of evolutionary theory or to include nonscientific ideas in biology courses, the NSTA maintains. The NSTA is an educational advocacy organization located in Arlington, Virginia.

As you read, consider the following questions:
1. What does the term "theory" mean in the world of science, according to the NSTA?
2. What are the main weaknesses of creation science, according to the authors?
3. According to the NSTA, which religious denominations opposed a bill to include creation science in public schools?

National Science Teachers Association, "NSTA Position Statement: The Teaching of Evolution," http://www.nsta.org/position. This position statement reprinted courtesy of the National Science Teachers Association, Arlington, VA.

The National Science Teachers Association (NSTA) strongly supports the position that evolution is a major unifying concept in science and should be included in the K–12 science education frameworks and curricula. Furthermore, if evolution is not taught, students will not achieve the level of scientific literacy they need. This position is consistent with that of the National Academies, the American Association for the Advancement of Science (AAAS), and many other scientific and educational organizations.

NSTA also recognizes that evolution has not been emphasized in science curricula in a manner commensurate to its importance because of official policies, intimidation of science teachers, the general public's misunderstanding of evolutionary theory, and a century of controversy. In addition, teachers are being pressured to introduce creationism, "creation science," and other nonscientific views, which are intended to weaken or eliminate the teaching of evolution.

Declarations

Within this context, NSTA recommends that

• Science curricula, state science standards, and teachers should emphasize evolution in a manner commensurate with its importance as a unifying concept in science and its overall explanatory power.

• Science teachers should not advocate any religious interpretations of nature and should be nonjudgmental about the personal beliefs of students.

• Policy makers and administrators should not mandate policies requiring the teaching of "creation science" or related concepts, such as so-called "intelligent design," "abrupt appearance," and "arguments against evolution." Administrators also should support teachers against pressure to promote nonscientific views or to diminish or eliminate the study of evolution.

• Administrators and school boards should provide support to teachers as they review, adopt, and implement curricula that emphasize evolution. This should include professional development to assist teachers in teaching evolution in a comprehensive and professional manner.

• Parental and community involvement in establishing

the goals of science education and the curriculum development process should be encouraged and nurtured in our democratic society. However, the professional responsibility of science teachers and curriculum specialists to provide students with quality science education should not be compromised by censorship, pseudoscience, inconsistencies, faulty scholarship, or unconstitutional mandates.

• Science textbooks shall emphasize evolution as a unifying concept. Publishers should not be required or volunteer to include disclaimers in textbooks that distort or misrepresent the methodology of science and the current body of knowledge concerning the nature and study of evolution.

—Adopted by the NSTA Board of Directors July 2003

The Nature of Science and Scientific Theories

Science is a method of explaining the natural world. It assumes that anything that can be observed or measured is amenable to scientific investigation. Science also assumes that the universe operates according to regularities that can be discovered and understood through scientific investigations. The testing of various explanations of natural phenomena for their consistency with empirical data is an essential part of the methodology of science. Explanations that are not consistent with empirical evidence or cannot be tested empirically are not a part of science. As a result, explanations of natural phenomena that are not based on evidence but on myths, personal beliefs, religious values, and superstitions are not scientific. Furthermore, because science is limited to explaining natural phenomena through the use of empirical evidence, it cannot provide religious or ultimate explanations.

The most important scientific explanations are called "theories." In ordinary speech, "theory" is often used to mean "guess" or "hunch," whereas in scientific terminology, a theory is a set of universal statements that explain some aspect of the natural world. Theories are powerful tools. Scientists seek to develop theories that

• are firmly grounded in and based upon evidence;
• are logically consistent with other well-established principles;
• explain more than rival theories; and

• have the potential to lead to new knowledge.

The body of scientific knowledge changes as new observations and discoveries are made. Theories and other explanations change. New theories emerge, and other theories are modified or discarded. Throughout this process, theories are formulated and tested on the basis of evidence, internal consistency, and their explanatory power.

Evolution as a Unifying Concept

Evolution in the broadest sense can be defined as the idea that the universe has a history: that change through time has taken place. If we look today at the galaxies, stars, the planet Earth, and the life on planet Earth, we see that things today are different from what they were in the past: galaxies, stars, planets, and life forms have evolved. Biological evolution refers to the scientific theory that living things share ancestors from which they have diverged; it is called "descent with modification." There is abundant and consistent evidence from astronomy, physics, biochemistry, geochronology, geology, biology, anthropology, and other sciences that evolution has taken place.

As such, evolution is a unifying concept for science. The *National Science Education Standards* recognizes that conceptual schemes such as evolution "unify science disciplines and provide students with powerful ideas to help them understand the natural world," and recommends evolution as one such scheme. In addition, *Benchmarks for Science Literacy* from AAAS's Project 2061, as well as other national calls for science reform, all name evolution as a unifying concept because of its importance across the disciplines of science. Scientific disciplines with a historical component, such as astronomy, geology, biology, and anthropology, cannot be taught with integrity if evolution is not emphasized.

There is no longer a debate among scientists about whether evolution has taken place. There is considerable debate about how evolution has taken place: What are the processes and mechanisms producing change, and what has happened specifically during the history of the universe? Scientists often disagree about their explanations. In any science, disagreements are subject to rules of evaluation. Scientific conclusions are tested by experiment and observation, and evolution, as with any aspect of theoretical science, is continually open to and subject to experimental and observational testing.

Flaws of the "Equal-Time" Argument

How do you respond when someone suggests that the fair thing to do is teach children about both evolution and creationism, and let them decide what to believe?

At its heart, the "equal-time" argument is substantially flawed. People who advocate it are basically saying we should teach that evolutionary theory—the idea that the universe changed through time, that the present is different from the past—is equal in weight to the idea that the whole universe came into being at one time and hasn't changed since then. You can't do that in a science class. You can only deal with scientific evidence. There is copious evidence to support that evolution has occurred, and no evidence that everything was created at once and hasn't changed. Why would we pretend that an idea that was created outside of science is science? That's not fair.

It's perfectly reasonable to expose children to religious views of origin, but it's not OK to advocate those views as empirical truth. And the place for those ideas is not in the science curriculum.

Eugenie Scott, interviewed by Leon Lynn, *Rethinking Schools*, Winter 1997–1998.

The importance of evolution is summarized as follows in the National Academy of Sciences publication *Teaching about Evolution and the Nature of Science:* "Few other ideas in science have had such a far-reaching impact on our thinking about ourselves and how we relate to the world."

Creationism and Other Nonscientific Views

The *National Science Education Standards* note that, "[e]xplanations of how the natural world changes based on myths, personal beliefs, religious values, mystical inspiration, superstition, or authority may be personally useful and socially relevant, but they are not scientific." Because science limits itself to natural explanations and not religious or ultimate ones, science teachers should neither advocate any religious interpretation of nature nor assert that religious interpretations of nature are not possible.

The word "creationism" has many meanings. In its broadest meaning, creationism is the idea that the universe is the consequence of something transcendent. Thus to Christians, Jews, and Muslims, God created; to the Navajo, the Hero Twins created; for Hindu Shaivites, the universe comes to exist as Shiva dances. In a narrower sense, "creationism" has come to mean "special creation": the doctrine that the universe and all that is in it was created by God in essentially its present form, at one time. The most common variety of special creationism asserts that

- the Earth is very young;
- life was created by God;
- life appeared suddenly;
- kinds of organisms have not changed since the creation; and
- different life forms were designed to function in particular settings.

This version of special creation is derived from a literal interpretation of Biblical Genesis. It is a specific, sectarian religious belief that is not held by all religious people. Many Christians and Jews believe that God created through the process of evolution. Pope John Paul II, for example, issued a statement in 1996 that reiterated the Catholic position that God created and affirmed that the evidence for evolution from many scientific fields is very strong.

"Creation science" is a religious effort to support special creationism through methods of science. Teachers are often pressured to include it or other related nonscientific views such as "abrupt appearance theory," "initial complexity theory," "arguments against evolution," or "intelligent design theory" when they teach evolution. Scientific creationist claims have been discredited by the available scientific evidence. They have no empirical power to explain the natural world and its diverse phenomena. Instead, creationists seek out supposed anomalies among many existing theories and accepted facts. Furthermore, "creation science" claims do not lead to new discoveries of scientific knowledge.

Legal Issues

Several judicial decisions have ruled on issues associated with the teaching of evolution and the imposition of mandates that "creation science" be taught when evolution is taught. The First Amendment of the Constitution requires that public institutions such as schools be religiously neutral; because "creation science" asserts a specific, sectarian religious view, it cannot be advocated in the public schools.

When Arkansas passed a law requiring "equal time" for "creation science" and evolution, the law was challenged in Federal District Court. Opponents of the bill included the religious leaders of the United Methodist, Episcopalian, Roman Catholic, African Methodist Episcopal, Presbyterian, and Southern Baptist churches, along with several educational organizations. After a full trial, the judge ruled that "creation science" did not qualify as a scientific theory (*McLean v. Arkansas Board of Education*, 529 F. Supp. 1255 [ED Ark. 1982]).

Louisiana's equal time law was challenged in court, and eventually reached the Supreme Court. In *Edwards v. Aguillard*, [482 U.S. 578 (1987)] the court determined that "creation science" was inherently a religious idea and to mandate or advocate it in the public schools would be unconstitutional. Other court decisions have upheld the right of a district to require that a teacher teach evolution and not teach "creation science" (*Webster v. New Lennox School District, #122*, 917 F.2d 1003 [7th Cir. 1990]; *Peloza v. Capistrano Unified School District*, 37 F.3d 517 [9th Cir. 1994]).

Some legislators and policy makers continue attempts to distort the teaching of evolution through mandates that would require teachers to teach evolution as "only a theory" or that require a textbook or lesson on evolution to be preceded by a disclaimer. Regardless of the legal status of these mandates, they are bad educational policy. Such policies have the effect of intimidating teachers, which may result in the de-emphasis or omission of evolution. As a consequence, the public will only be further confused about the nature of scientific theories. Furthermore, if students learn less about evolution, science literacy itself will suffer.

6

"[The] rich and wonderful debate [on evolution] . . . does not take place, by and large, among biology teachers in K–12 classrooms."

The Avoidance of Creationism in Science Courses Stifles Debate

Patrick Glynn

Students miss out when science teachers reject alternative notions concerning evolutionary theory, argues Patrick Glynn in the following viewpoint. While certain fundamentalist religious claims about the origin of life, such as creationism, have been largely discredited by scientists, the avoidance of *any* dissenting views keeps students from learning about revolutionary theories, Glynn maintains. In their efforts to keep creationism out of science curricula, educators have stifled legitimate ideas, including the notion that evolution of the universe is the result of intelligent design. Glynn is associate director of the George Washington University for Communitarian Policy Studies and the author of *God: The Evidence.*

As you read, consider the following questions:
1. In what way has evolutionary science encroached on religion, in Glynn's opinion?
2. What is "intelligent design theory," according to the author?
3. How has information theory revolutionized ideas about the nature of life, according to Glynn?

Patrick Glynn, "Monkey on Our Backs," *National Review*, vol. 51, September 13, 1999, p. 42. Copyright © 1999 by National Review, Inc., 215 Lexington Ave., New York, NY 10016. Reproduced by permission.

Critics have decried the Kansas Board of Education's [1999] vote against evolution as a throwback to the 19th century.[1] In truth, though, both sides of the evolution-creationism debate are locked in a 19th-century quarrel, seemingly oblivious to 20th-century scientific developments that have rendered much of their argument obsolete. While the "ol' time religion" and Biblical literalism of Kansas board members have invited great scorn, many of their opponents in the evolution camp share a naively positivistic view of science, nearly as fundamentalist, in its own way, as the beliefs of creationists.

Not that anyone is likely to construe the Kansas board's decision to strike evolution from the state's required curriculum as a public-relations victory for evangelicalism. By allying themselves with so-called "scientific creationists" or "young-earth theorists," the board members did much to discredit more legitimate critiques of Darwin. While one can respect the piety of a person whose literal understanding of the Book of Genesis leads him to claim that the earth is no more than 10,000 years old, that individual should hardly be surprised if the world at large fails to regard his views as scientific. No less an authority than St. Augustine cautioned Christians against quoting the Bible as a science text and warned that by doing so they would tend to render their religion laughable in the eyes of more knowledgeable people. The Kansas board members fell into this trap.

Science Encroaching on Religion

But if the Kansans allowed religion to encroach all too clumsily on science, they were reacting in part to an evolutionary science that has too often encroached on religion. In 1997, Phillip Johnson, the University of California law professor and outspoken critic of Darwin, drew attention to the then-official definition of "evolution" promulgated by the National Association of Biology Teachers:

"The diversity of life on earth is the outcome of evolution: an unsupervised, impersonal, unpredictable and natural pro-

1. In 2001 the Kansas Board of Education voted to restore evolution to the state's science curriculum.

cess of temporal descent with genetic modification that is affected by natural selection, chance, historical contingencies and changing environments."

Modern geology has established persuasively that the earth is a good deal older than 10,000 years (the current estimate is 4.5 billion). Most scientists accept that the fossil record shows evidence of macroevolution—i.e., the emergence of new species—and common descent. But the evidence is a long way from supporting the claim that the process was "unsupervised, impersonal" or even based solely on "chance." That is not a conclusion based on data. It is rather the assumption of most biologists going in.

The board of the biology teachers' association reluctantly agreed to drop the words "unsupervised" and "impersonal" from their definition after receiving a letter of protest from the eminent religion scholar Huston Smith and Notre Dame philosopher Alvin Plantinga, who pointed out that while the fossil record may provide evidence for evolution, it fails to establish whether evolution "is or isn't directed by God." But the underlying logic of the teachers' definition—the implication that all life and species can be explained solely by chance mechanisms—remains the official position of the profession, indeed its central tenet.

No Middle Ground?

All of which helps to explain why a middle ground in this controversy, while seemingly available in theory, has proved so elusive in practice. The *Washington Post* editorialized evenhandedly enough about the Kansas decision, noting that evolution is a "reality," "no matter how inconvenient," and adding: "This is not to say that there is no significant debate over its mode and character. There is, in fact, a rich and wonderful one." This rich and wonderful debate, however, does not take place, by and large, among biology teachers in K–12 classrooms.

The draft science requirements rejected by the Kansas board had two striking features. First, the draft contained a remarkably heavy dose of evolution, more than most of us middle-aged folks remember from our own school days. Second, it presented evolutionary biology in a manner suggesting an utter absence of controversy within or about the field. The document included a footnote to the effect that students were required to "understand" rather than profess "belief" in evolutionary theory. But the curriculum made no provision for the presentation of dissenting views. The notion that there exists legitimate disagreement, scientific or even philosophical, about evolution was nowhere suggested.

Evolution Is Speculative Science

A persistent criticism of science instruction is that evolution is often taught as "dogma" or as a "just so story." Mere scenarios of major evolutionary transformations are often presented as though they were "historical" observations, when neither the events nor their mechanism is actually known or perhaps even knowable. While some teachers do emphasize the theoretical nature of evolution, rarely is a critical view taken of this highly speculative field of science. As a result, the student and even the teacher are often led to conclude that there is no substantive criticism of evolutionary ideas among professional scientists, but such is hardly the case.

David N. Menton, *Teaching Origins in Public Schools*, 1991.

Indeed, experience has shown that it can be risky for a high-school instructor to explore what the *Post* calls this "rich and wonderful" debate. Recently the *Christian Science Monitor* carried a story about a Minnesota biology teacher, Rodney LeVake, who raised questions about the validity of natural selection and introduced his class to "intelligent design theory"—the position advocated by some scientists that the order intrinsic in the universe provides empirical evidence of design or creation. For his troubles LeVake was barred by the local school board from teaching biology the next year.

Interestingly, the rejected Kansas curriculum also featured a component on cosmic evolution, including the big-bang theory. But nowhere did it mention an issue that has generated a vast literature in cosmology—the anthropic principle, or the mystery of the "cosmic coincidences" in the universe, which a number of scientists argue strongly suggest the existence of design. (Unfortunately, the majority of the Kansas board discarded the cosmic-evolution component of the curriculum as well.)

Students Are Missing Out

Part of the difficulty here is legal and constitutional. The Supreme Court has ruled against the teaching of creationism in public schools, and any discussion of intelligent design in a public-school classroom might border dangerously on teaching religion. But as a result of these legal restrictions, supposed or real, and the conventional mindset of the biology profession, students are missing out on a major revolution in the sciences, which may, ironically enough, hold a solution to the evolution-creationism deadlock.

The most interesting challenges to the 19th-century Darwinian understanding of evolution have come not from biology, but from new 20th-century disciplines—in particular, astrophysics and information theory. In reconstructing the evolution of the cosmos, astrophysicists have discovered a universe that seems mysteriously and intricately preprogrammed for life. Regardless of how life originated, this preprogramming seems almost incompatible with mere chance.

In addition, information theory, in combination with molecular biology, has revolutionized our idea of life. In particular, it has led to the insight that life is not simply matter, but matter plus information. DNA is in effect a "message" coded in matter. Matter can carry information; it cannot, so far as we know, create information. The question therefore arises, Where does the information come from?

In Darwin's day it was commonly believed that the laws of biology would eventually be reduced to the laws of chemistry, and the laws of chemistry in turn to the laws of physics. But now it has been established that the simplest version of DNA contains more information than is contained in all the laws of chemistry and physics. So such reductionism—a goal at the heart of the Darwinian project—is no longer conceivable.

These are the issues that would light a fire in students and open minds. But thanks to a legacy of bitter legal and constitutional conflict, and to the doctrinal rigidities of the biology profession, students may be exposed to "current events" in every field but the life sciences, as our schools remain locked in a war between two 19th-century fundamentalisms, one religious, the other scientific.

Periodical Bibliography

The following articles have been selected to supplement the diverse views presented in this chapter.

Julie Benyo	"A Revolutionary Attempt to Bolster the Teaching of Evolution," *Curriculum Review*, September 2002.
Facts On File News Services	"Character Education," *Issues and Controversies On File*, October 25, 2002.
Tim Giago	"We Knew Jerry Falwell and Pat Robertson Long Before They Were Born," *Lakota Nation Journal*, March 8, 2000.
Dahleen Glanton	"Ten Commandments Become Weapon in Church-State Battle," *Houston Chronicle*, December 16, 2001.
Andrew Goldstein	"The Pros and Cons of the Bush Character Education Plan," *Time*, July 6, 2001.
Stephen Goode	"The Education of Good Character," *Insight on the News*, March 15, 1999.
James Davison Hunter	"Leading Children Beyond Good and Evil," *First Things*, May 2000.
Wendy Kaminer	"Religion, Public Schools, and Gray Areas," *Free Inquiry*, Summer 2001.
Gerald A. Larue	"Science, Religion, and Public School Education," *Humanist*, May/June 1998.
John Leo	"Professors Who See No Evil," *U.S. News & World Report*, July 22, 2002.
Kathleen Manzo	"Debating the Decalogue," *Education Week*, August 8, 2001.
Warren A. Nord	"Religion-Free Texts: Getting an Illiberal Education," *Christian Century*, July 14, 1999.
Eugenie C. Scott	"Not (Just) in Kansas Anymore," *Science*, May 5, 2000.
Svi Shapiro	"The New Crisis in Education," *Tikkun*, September 2000.
Christina Hoff Sommers	"Are We Living in a Moral Stone Age?" *USA Today Magazine*, March 1999.
Gregory A. Valde	"Schools Without Souls: Moral Community and Public School," *Tikkun*, September 1999.

CHAPTER 4

How Could Public Education Be Improved?

Chapter Preface

With the passage of the No Child Left Behind (NCLB) Act in 2002, U.S. public schools now must ensure that all eighth-grade students are proficient in math and reading skills by the year 2014. To attain this goal, the NCLB has established a variety of incentives and sanctions to encourage school systems and states to take effective action. Many school districts are currently making critical choices about how they will use the federal funding that NCLB provides to boost the performance levels of teachers as well as students.

Since states must prove that they are making measurable progress toward the NCLB goal, many schools are monitoring student performance by giving standardized tests more frequently. These tests, which usually measure math and verbal skills, have created a renewed emphasis on traditional teaching methods in many school districts. Traditional forms of instruction, also referred to as "back to basics" teaching, emphasize memorization, recitation, drills, and structured, fact-based learning. Some educators contend that these techniques especially benefit economically disadvantaged students with serious academic deficiencies. Research suggests, moreover, that traditional methods significantly boost student performance. According to a University of Wisconsin study, writes commentator Marvin Olasky, "Teachers in higher-achieving first-grade classrooms emphasized basic skills and processes through modeling, drill, and practice. They preferred highly structured, goal-directed classrooms with established routines." In contrast, teachers in lower-achieving classrooms tend to believe that basic skills are secondary to the pleasure of learning. "They preferred 'child-centered experiential learning, in which the teacher serves as a facilitator' and generally managed students in a 'permissive and inconsistent' manner," states Olasky.

Critics of traditional methods, however, maintain that back-to-basics teaching imposes an impersonal, one-size-fits-all learning style on students. Many teachers argue that while rote memorization and multiple-choice testing may teach students *what* to think, they do not teach them *how* to think. Progressive teaching methods, on the other hand, incorporate personalized instruction group activities, hands-on learning, and experience-based knowledge to develop students' capacity for astute, probing thought. According to school administrator Deborah Meier, progressive techniques result in critical thinkers who ask:

1. How do we know what we think we know? What's our evidence? How credible is it?
2. Whose viewpoint are we hearing, reading, seeing? What other viewpoints might there be if we changed our position?
3. How is one thing connected to another? Is there a pattern here?
4. How else might it have been? What if? Supposing that?
5. What difference does it make? Who cares?

While progressivists and traditionalists may seem to be at odds, there are many educators who believe that schools need to incorporate both kinds of instructional methods. Traditionalist instruction in basic skills in the early grades, they argue, should lay the groundwork for the more complex and less rigidly structured learning that older students need. Moreover, disciplined learning of facts can be combined with activities that foster knowledge integration and insightful thinking. "These two traditions represent the best we know about teaching and learning," states David B. Ackerman, CEO of The Learning Navigator, which provides multifaceted support for learners. In the most outstanding schools, he argues, "both the progressive and the traditional strands intertwine, reinforcing and amplifying one another."

As U.S. schools strive to improve student performance in the coming years, debates on teaching styles and instructional techniques are likely to intensify. In the following chapter, authors discuss additional policies and issues central to the goal of improving public education.

"To realize success, you must measure it."

Standardized Testing and Assessment Improve Education

Don W. Hooper

In the following viewpoint Don W. Hooper maintains that educational systems that use objective standards to measure student achievement are highly effective. Schools that set predetermined goals for student success and that monitor progress through standardized testing boost academic performance, he contends. In Hooper's opinion, well-planned accountability systems that emphasize assessment, incentives for improvement, and community involvement can improve education. Hooper is president of the American Association of School Administrators.

As you read, consider the following questions:
1. What kind of educational system is more likely to produce lasting failure, in Hooper's opinion?
2. What percentage of students in the Fort Bend, Texas, Independent School District passed standardized reading tests in 2001?
3. According to the American Association of School Administrators, what nine attributes should state-level accountability systems include?

Don W. Hooper, "Accountability for Student Success," *School Administrator*, vol. 58, December 2001, p. 38. Copyright © 2001 by the American Association of School Administrators. All rights reserved. Reproduced by permission.

Imagine you are a 4th-grader in a classroom where children seem happy, the teacher seems relaxed, parents are actively involved in school activities and, as far as you know, your education program is in good hands. You rarely may know the objective, but you take the normal teacher-made test and the annual achievement test, and as long as you are making good grades in class you aren't concerned about the rest of the world.

Some distance away your cousin, also a 4th-grader whose parents are similarly involved in school is in a totally different learning environment. The children in that classroom also are happy. The atmosphere while not relaxed is energized because the teacher, the students and the parents all know the learning objectives and goals and the assessment that will verify their success.

Promoting Maximum Learning

This second learning environment is one focused on preparation for high-level performance and the resulting exhilaration one feels from having succeeded. Failure or success on a test is merely the benchmark that reflects your cousin's current progress, not labels that stigmatize her capabilities. In short, this is a system that guarantees the youngster's likelihood of success.

In this scenario, both students trust they are experiencing a high-quality educational program. Both are enjoying their experiences. However, the philosophies behind the two educational systems differ greatly. Which student will longitudinal data show is not well prepared for life, and which is far ahead in the quest for making a living and succeeding at life?

The first student is part of an educational system geared to avoid high-stakes testing and the other is in a system that monitors progress systematically against predetermined standards. Assuming the standards are set properly, I believe the first student will have a happenstance opportunity for success, whereas the second student will have a significant opportunity for success—because the system wins every time.

This should not be a debate about high-stakes testing or a crusade to demonize accountability for results in K–12 education. This is about the responsibility of public school leadership to design and implement a system to promote maximum learning by students.

Raising Achievement Levels

To realize success, you must measure it. When you measure it, regardless of the day or time of year, there will be consequences. Some will pass and some will fail. Both outcomes should be used to calibrate the system of teaching and learning to further the students' learning. The likelihood of lasting failure is greater in a system that is not organized around predetermined objectives, where the objectives are not measured effectively and are not used to adjust how the system operates.

I have witnessed firsthand what an accountability system can do to raise the achievement and development levels for all—and I do mean all—students. My district, Fort Bend Independent School District, the state's 10th largest, is a Texas Education Agency "Recognized" school district. Our more than 56,000 students come from 25 countries and speak 65 different languages at home. We are very diverse.

A Measure, Not a Cure

Tests are vital tools for measuring student progress and for identifying where students'—and schools'—achievement can be improved. But a test is a thermometer, not a treatment. More and more testing is not a "cure" for poor student achievement. That can only be solved through a comprehensive program of lower class size, highly qualified teachers, appropriate instructional materials and adequate school facilities.

Good tests, used properly, will help us understand how children are doing, help direct resources to those in need, and reassure parents that their children are getting a broad and rigorous education.

Sandra Feldman, *National Journal*, June 2, 2001.

Since 1995 the passage rates in reading of our African American students increased from 67.6 percent passing to 88.1 percent. Hispanic students' passage rates rose from 69.3 percent to 85.7 percent. White students went from 91.9 percent to 97.4 percent passing, and our economically disadvantaged students' scores rose from 67.6 percent to 83 percent passing.

Similar results have been achieved in mathematics and writing. Combined passage rates for all Fort Bend students tested in spring 2001 are as follows: reading, 92.7 percent; math, 92.5 percent; and writing, 91.8 percent. Ninety-three percent of our students are reading on grade level by 3rd grade. These are our Texas Assessment of Academic Skills test results. Additionally, our National Assessment of Educational Progress [NAEP] scores are up, and our increasing ACT and SAT scores surpass state and national averages.

In addition, the percentage of Fort Bend students who take the college-entrance tests, including minority students, is among the highest in the country (85 percent).

Strong Accountability Systems

I cite these statistics not to brag about my school district, although our board, staff, students and community are rightfully proud of our accomplishments. At a time when some demonize accountability systems that measure student progress, my point here is to illustrate how others use these systems to significantly increase student progress.

According to Secretary of Education Rod Paige, the performance of 4th-grade students in Texas on the NAEP equals or exceeds non-minority scores in some other states. That not only closes the original achievement gap, it also creates another one where the white student scores of those states are below the minority student scores in Texas, where we have a statewide accountability system.

During my term as AASA [American Association of School Administrators] president, I have had the opportunity to meet with leading educators nationally and internationally. Most of those who speak the loudest against strong accountability systems are those who have the least experience with them. Or perhaps they have had experience with poorly designed systems. Most of those with extensive experience working with strong accountability systems are the strongest advocates. They know firsthand that the systems improve student success.

Our role is to properly design systems that will lead to

successful outcomes for students. Properly designed systems must be built over time. The Texas journey has been a 20-year experience. Positive results can be seen in just a few years. However, patience, plus the engagement of all stakeholders, is necessary for proper system design.

Resolving to Succeed

[In the summer of 2001], the AASA Resolutions Committee drafted the following accountability resolution . . . :

AASA supports accurate state-level accountability systems designed, developed, measured and reported in order to improve the academic achievement of each student. We believe such systems should include:

1. A development process that includes educational leaders, business leaders and broad-based community involvement.
2. Multiple measures of student success.
3. A common body of essential knowledge and skills developed by all stakeholders in each state.
4. Funding for intervention programs and services necessary for improving student achievement.
5. Early childhood education programs in collaboration with other agencies that provide readiness for preschoolers.
6. A solid infrastructure for continuous improvement that includes curriculum audits, alignment of the written, taught and tested curriculum and professional development.
7. Comparisons of school or district performance based on data from comparable districts or schools.
8. Incentives for improvement gains or consistent high performance and sanctions for continued failure to meet established goals and standards.
9. A monitoring process that accounts for normal variation by using valid and reliable statistical measures.

Suffice it to say, I am a proponent of well-designed systems that actually do something for students. My theme . . . as AASA president is "Shaping the Future, One Child at a Time." It can be done. It is being done. And you can do it, too!

"Standard measurements of learning are inadequate."

Standardized Testing and Assessment Do Not Improve Education

Matthew Miltich

Assessment and standardized tests should not take priority in education, argues Matthew Miltich in the following viewpoint. Although objective measurements of learning are useful, they are no replacement for dedicated teachers who encourage students to pursue and cherish their education, Miltich writes. True learning is a deeply personal and enriching experience that ultimately cannot be measured through standardized evaluation, he concludes. Miltich teaches English at Itasca Community College near Grand Rapids, Minnesota.

As you read, consider the following questions:
1. What personal experience helped Miltich to see that teaching and learning cannot be separated from one's life outside the classroom?
2. According to Miltich, why are most teachers wary of the assessment movement in education?
3. Who is ultimately responsible for learning, in the author's opinion?

Matthew Miltich, "'Teaching and Learning Are Personal'; the Death of His Son Took This Professor Back to His Students—and Away from Traditional Assessments," *NEA Today*, vol. 20, March 2002, p. 7. Copyright © 2002 by the National Education Association of the United States. Reproduced by permission.

During the spring quarter of 1996, immediately after the death of my son Andrew, I found that when I was alone in my office on campus or at home, I could not read student papers from my learners at Itasca Community College, where I teach English.

I couldn't focus, couldn't concentrate my thoughts upon my learners' words on paper, or even make myself believe in the importance of grades or other prescriptive measures of their learning.

Sometimes, my vision blurred by grief, I couldn't even see the words my students had written. I could, however, see the students. Each one of them seemed to me as dear as my own child, so I had no trouble being with them, or reading their work and talking with them about their reading and other school work when they were with me.

In my composition classes, I worked with one person at a time offering individual help with writing.

I abandoned written examinations and instead questioned each learner individually. Each examination became a private conversation and each conscientious learner told me more about her or his learning than I'd ever discovered in written exams.

Learning Is Personal

My experiences that quarter taught me more deeply the lesson I'd been learning one class day at a time for more than 20 years: Teaching and learning are personal, individual, and unique—and also inseparable from who we are and from our lives away from the classroom.

Years have passed since the death of my boy, and I can read student writing again and grade exams, both of which I consider honorable activities. But my conviction has deepened that every experience of learning, like each learner, is singular. I've concluded that for me and my learners, standard measurements of learning are inadequate.

Now, I find myself in direct conflict with the "assessment" movement in education. I disagree with the assumptions of this movement, and I'm suspicious of its advocates.

I disagree that assessment should assume a priority role in education. The evangelists in the movement offer it as a kind of panacea. I see it as a distraction that diverts our attention from more critical, more primary issues.

"WOLFGANG! MIKE! STOP WASTING TIME! YOU SHOULD BE DOING PRACTICE DRILLS FOR THE STATE EXAMS!!"

Horsey. © 2000 by *Seattle Post-Intelligencer*. Reproduced by permission.

We must provide for our learners. Measurement is no substitute for nourishment. Advocates for assessment like to talk about nurturing students and about learning communities, but they end by focusing on measurement, data gathering, and quantification. Moreover, assessment programs absorb resources that otherwise might provide students with truly enriched and enriching learning experiences.

What Students Need

Students need good instruction and good instructors. The assessment movement promises to improve instruction; but assessment has failed to capture the imagination of most teachers because the promise of improved instruction can't come true if assessment is the means for making it happen. Instruction will improve when administrators make careers in education more attractive and provide better support and greater access to professional development.

The assessment movement has promised to make us more

accountable by providing tools for reporting measurable outcomes—a way to prove our worth and to hold us responsible for the learning of our students. Standardized tests, charts, scoring grids, rubrics, and assessment tools are promoted as the means by which we can quantify and report this learning.

What this promise fails to account for is that, for good or ill, no matter how well we teach, learning rests finally with the learner—and this is as it should be.

No more important moment comes for a learner than that in which she is struck, forcefully and clearly, by the notion that she and only she is responsible for her learning. No quantification can account for this revelation, but learners know when it occurs, and afterward they value worthy instructors as guides and allies in their learning experiences. Such an immeasurable outcome is worth more than any portfolio of objective data.

While objective evaluation of learning is important, learning can go on without it. No "assessment program" can take the place of energized, passionate faculty who love their disciplines and their learners and learning itself.

"We are insisting on high standards and high achievement for every school in every corner of America."

The No Child Left Behind Act Is Improving Education

George W. Bush

The No Child Left Behind Act, signed into law in 2002, mandates that all students completing the eighth grade by the year 2014 be proficient in academic skills. To achieve this goal, the law requires states to submit their own accountability plans that result in annual measurable gains in student performance. In the following viewpoint, excerpted from a speech delivered on June 10, 2003, George W. Bush maintains that the new law is creating significant educational progress: Extra funding for schools in low-income areas, basic skills education, frequent testing and assessment of student progress, enhanced teacher training, and tutoring are enabling all American children to receive a high-quality education. Bush is the forty-third president of the United States.

As you read, consider the following questions:

1. What is the educational budget for the year 2004, according to Bush?
2. According to the author, what is the "core" of the No Child Left Behind Act?
3. In Bush's opinion, why is it important for local communities to take the lead in improving public schools?

George W. Bush, televised address, Washington, DC, June 10, 2003.

Welcome to the White House and the beautiful Rose Garden. I want to thank you for coming today to help us mark progress, significant progress, toward making sure our public schools meet our objective, which is every single child in America gets a high-quality education.

[In 2002], I had the honor of signing into law some historic reforms. The No Child Left Behind Act sets a clear objective for American education. Every child in every school must be performing at grade level in the basic subjects that are key to all learning, reading and math. The ambitious goal is the most fundamental duty of every single school, and it must and it will be fulfilled.

In order to ensure this goal is met, the No Child Left Behind Act requires every State in our country to submit an accountability plan that leads to measurable gains in student performance. As of today [June 10, 2003], all of the States, plus Puerto Rico and the District of Columbia, have now submitted those plans. And that's why we're meeting.

The era of low expectations and low standards is ending; a time of great hopes and proven results is arriving. And together, we are keeping a pledge: Every child in America will learn, and no child will be left behind. . . .

Focusing on the Problem

For too many years, education reform seemed like a losing battle. Fads came and fads went while students were passed from grade to grade, no matter what they did or did not learn. And as a result, national tests showed that fewer than 1 in 3 fourth graders were reading well and that only 4 in 10 high school seniors were skilled at reading. Because we were just simply shuffling kids through the system, we began to pay a serious price.

But fortunately, we recognized the problem, and we acted. I say "we"—it's not only Republicans but Democrats. All of us came together to focus on a significant problem for our country. We are now directly challenging the soft bigotry of low expectations. Under the No Child Left Behind Act, every student in this country will be held to high standards, and every school will be held accountable for results. Teachers will get the training they need to help their students achieve. Parents will get the information and choices they need to make sure their children are learning. And together we will bring the promise of quality education to every child in America.

Part of the answer is funding, and we are meeting our obligations here in Washington, DC. The Federal Government is investing more money in elementary and secondary education than at any other time in American history. The budget for [2004] boosts education funding to $53.1 billion and an increase of nearly $11 billion since I took office. And it wasn't all that long ago that I took office. Funding for Title I, a program that helps our most disadvantaged students, has increased 33 percent to $11.6 billion. And since I took office, we've tripled the amount we're spending on effective reading programs to more than $1 billion.

At the Federal level, we are putting money into the system. It is also important for our fellow citizens to understand that there is money available for States to put in accountability systems, for States to train teachers in the methods that work, and for States to provide extra help to students who need it.

Asking for Results

But it's also important to recognize that pouring money into systems that do not teach and refuse to change will not help our children. We help children by measuring the educational progress of every single child and by insisting on change when progress is not made. We're spending more money on schools, but the change is we're now asking for results. And those results must be proven, and those results must be measured every single year.

Success comes when we've got strong leadership in our schools, leaders who seek the truth, leaders who are willing to confront reality, and leadership who believes in the worth of every single child. And we have such a leader with us today. Linda Reksten is with us today. Linda is the principal of Disney Elementary School in Burbank, California. It's a Title I school where half the students are not fluent in English and nearly two-thirds come from low-income families.

Four years ago, her students scored at the 40th and 44th

percentiles for reading comprehension and math on the State tests. And her school wound up on a list of underperforming schools. At first, Linda said she and her teachers felt powerless, felt overwhelmed. But they overcame their discouragement and got to work.

REACHING THE TOP

Eleanor Mill. © 2001 by Mill NewsArt Syndicate. Reproduced by permission.

And here's what Disney School did. They began a rigorous testing program to measure the progress of every child several times a year. Teachers who had initially been skeptical of the tests—and I'm sure the State leaders here have heard of that skepticism before—learned how to use test results to tailor their lessons plans and to make sure every child excelled. Morale went up. Discipline problems were down. And [in 2002], Disney students scored at the 58th percentile in reading comprehension and the 71st percentile in math. And that is tremendous progress.

And let me tell you what Linda said. She said, "It is this constant assessment that tells us what to do next. Once we have the test data and we know where the gaps are, we go after the gaps. We know where every child is." Linda is right. She has shown what works in education. She is the model of education reform. I'm proud you're here. Thank you for your leadership, and thank you for your heart.

The Goal Is Progress

The core of the No Child Left Behind legislation is that every child must be tested on the basics, starting early, because testing shows what children are learning and where they need help. We also need to train the teachers in scientifically proven methods of teaching the basics so that their students can make progress. And if the basics are not being taught and our children are not meeting standards, schools must be held to account. There must be a consequence. The status quo, if a school is mediocre, is not acceptable.

We're making good progress in terms of the implementation of our accountability systems. In the past 5 months, we have approved the accountability plans of 33 States, plus the District of Columbia and Puerto Rico. And today we mark an historic milestone of accountability: This morning, Secretary [of Education Rod] Paige has approved the plans of 17 more States, bringing us to a total of 100 percent of the accountability plans in place.

I want to thank the Secretary again and his staff and education chiefs for helping this Nation make great progress when it comes to education reform. Keep in mind that in January of 2001, only 11 States were in compliance with a 1994 education law. Every State, plus Puerto Rico and the District, are now complying with the No Child Left Behind Act after one year.

A Culture of Achievement

Educators are embracing a new level of accountability, which is creating a new culture for our Nation's schools, a culture of achievement, a culture of results over process. In this new culture, accountability plans are driving reform. They contain timelines and projections to show how the States will bring all students up to grade level in reading and math by the year 2014. All students will be tested—tests designed by the States, not the Federal Government. Schools are required to disaggregate the testing data, separating the results by race and background to make sure all groups of children are learning. All schools must release report cards with these results to the parents and to the public, so we know which schools are succeeding and which schools are not.

Though the plans have these common elements, each plan is unique because each State and its communities are unique. Local people are getting the tools they need to find out if children are learning and if their schools are working. Local people are charting the path to excellence, and that is important because local people know what is best for their own children and their own schools.

The development of these plans involved a lot of hard work. Governors stepped up to the line, along with their education chiefs. I also want to thank the principals and teachers and parents on the frontlines who are working so hard to improve our public schools. Instead of throwing up your hands in despair, you decided to challenge the status quo and to help each child. On behalf of the Nation, I want to thank all who are involved in America's public schools, all who demand excellence, for your service to our country.

The Next Phase

And now we look forward to the next phase of school reform. The law requires every State to release a list of its schools in need of improvement before the start of the school year. The schools on those lists are immediately eligible for State assistance that can help them improve. The school remains on the list for 2 years. Parents will have the option of moving their children to other public schools in the same district. If a school stays on the list for 3 years, a parent will be given a choice of tutoring programs with proven track records, programs in which they can enroll their children at no cost.

The No Child Left Behind Act gives parents and students alternatives when schools do not measure up. Some of those schools will undoubtedly have to make difficult choices. That's okay. Remember what's at stake. When a student passes from grade to grade without knowing how to read and write, add and subtract, the damage can last a lifetime. We must not tolerate a system that just gives up on a child early. We must not tolerate tired excuses. We must challenge persistent failure. And that is precisely what this Nation is going to do. We are insisting on high standards and high achievement for every school in every corner of America because we have a fundamental belief that every child can learn in this country.

It's an exciting time for American education; it really is. We're facing challenges, but we have the blueprint for success. The No Child Left Behind Act charts the way for a better tomorrow. We've also got a greater advantage than the law. We have got the will and the character of the American people. Parents and teachers and principals and education chiefs are making good on our promise to leave no child left behind. We will continue to stand with them as they help the next generation realize the greatness of our country.

And we do live in a great country, a country of great values, a country of hope, a country that believes in the best for every single citizen who lives in our land.

May God bless your work, and may God continue to bless the United States of America.

> "*The legislation is exacerbating, not solving,
> the real problems that cause many children
> to be left behind.*"

The No Child Left Behind Act Is Not Improving Education

Monty Neill

The 2002 No Child Left Behind Act, which requires schools to make measurable yearly progress toward empowering all students with basic academic skills, is deeply flawed, argues Monty Neill in the following viewpoint. According to Neill, the law places too much emphasis on standardized tests, causing teachers to focus on test preparation rather than on real learning. The law also places unrealistic demands on schools serving low-income students, the author points out. If these schools fail to raise test scores at the rate the law mandates, teachers may be forced to abandon instructional methods that worked for them. Moreover, an emphasis on quantifiable progress creates an unhealthy antagonism among teachers, parents, and communities as schools struggle to avoid the "failing" label. Neill is executive of the National Center for Fair and Open Testing in Cambridge, Massachusetts.

As you read, consider the following questions:

1. According to Neill, what is the difference between a norm-referenced test and a criterion-referenced test?
2. How does living in an impoverished environment affect one's capacity to learn, according to the author?
3. What suggestions does Neill have for reforming public school education?

Monty Neill, "Low Expectations and Less Learning: The Problem with the No Child Left Behind Act," *Social Education*, vol. 67, September 2003, p. 281.

"No Child Left Behind," the name of the federal Elementary and Secondary Education Act (ESEA), describes a worthy goal for our nation. Tragically, the legislation is exacerbating, not solving, the real problems that cause many children to be left behind.

Of course, we all want to achieve improved student performance in schools where performance by many measures has been low. However, in many states the gauge of student learning is being reduced to reading and math test scores. As a result, crucial social studies disciplines—such as history and civics—are being squeezed to the margins of the curricula because those subjects are either not tested or tested less than others. In the tested subjects (including social studies when tested), many schools limit instruction to the material that appears on the exams. Education is being damaged, especially in low-income and minority schools, as students are coached to pass narrow tests rather than learn a rich curriculum to prepare them for life in the twenty-first century.

The Problem with High-Stakes Testing

The emphasis placed by "No Child Left Behind" on high-stakes testing for schools reinforces the policies of nearly half the states to make major decisions about students on the basis of standardized tests. Yet the Standards for Educational and Psychological Testing state that tests should not be used as the sole basis for high-stakes decisions such as graduation or grade promotion.

The current emphasis on standardized tests flies in the face of our existing knowledge of what those tests can and cannot do. While test scores offer numbers that seem very precise, they are only estimates of a student's knowledge. Just as nationwide polls that survey public attitudes always have a margin of error, so too do standardized tests. On a traditional norm-referenced standardized test, a score at the 50th percentile means it is quite likely that a test-taker falls somewhere between the 44th and 56th percentile of students taking the test. While this particular test puts him or her right in the middle, different tests would likely result in a judgment of either "above average" or "below average."

For such reasons, efforts to measure the progress of schools with these tests are fraught with error. Because of random fluctuations, Massachusetts schools receiving awards one year for increases in their test scores have almost never been given awards the next year. In many cases, the scores of "award-winning" schools have actually declined. In a study of North Carolina, researchers Thomas Kane and Douglas Staiger found that a school that attempted to predict next year's scores would obtain a more accurate estimate by looking at the state's average school score change rather than by looking at changes in its own scores over the previous four years.

An Elusive Pursuit

As state budgets around the country are slashed to accommodate the expense of the war on terror, the pursuit of educational opportunity for all seems ever more elusive. While standardized tests are supposed to be used to diagnose problems and facilitate individual or institutional improvement, too often they have been used to close or penalize precisely the schools that most need help; or, results have been used to track students into separate programs that benefit the few but not the many. The implementation of gifted classes with better student-teacher ratios and more substantial resources often triggers an unhealthy and quite bitter competition for those unnaturally narrowed windows of opportunity. How much better it would be to have more public debate about why the pickings are so slim to begin with. In any event, it is no wonder there is such intense national anxiety just now, a fantastical hunger for children who speak in complete sentences by the age of six months.

Patricia J. Williams, *Nation*, April 22, 2002.

Another problem with standardized tests is that many of them are norm-referenced rather than criterion-referenced. In a criterion-referenced test, an attempt is made to measure whether the test-taker has sufficient knowledge or skills required for proficiency in a particular task. A driving test is an example: a person passes or fails based on his or her knowledge and skill. Whether one person passes or fails does not depend on how many others are able to pass the test. A criterion-referenced test focuses on what a student is expected to know and is designed to gauge whether a student has achieved the standards or learned the curriculum he or she has presumably been taught.

Most standardized tests, in contrast, are norm-referenced. Tests of this kind are oriented toward testing how students perform in relation to other students. By design, about half of all students will be declared "above average" and about half will be declared "below average." Such tests are designed to sort and rank large numbers of students in comparison to each other. While the majority of state tests now purport to be "criterion-referenced," most are made using the same technology as norm-referenced tests. Thus, they incorporate the same emphasis on sorting and ranking.

Existing state exams also fail to adequately represent or measure a high-quality curriculum. Focusing mainly on multiple-choice and short-answer items, the tests foster rote learning and drill-and-kill instruction. Thus, the quality of teaching will not be improved by testing. Rather, teachers will merely "add on a layer of test preparation" to what they already teach, or replace teaching with test coaching.

Unrealistic Demands

The federally-mandated accountability provisions also will contribute to undermining, rather than improving school quality. Many schools will fail to meet the unrealistic demands imposed by ESEA's "adequate yearly progress" provision, which says all students must attain the "proficient" level on state assessments of reading and math by 2014. Virtually no schools serving low-income children will clear the arbitrary hurdles. Many improving schools will be declared "failing" and forced to drop approaches to teaching that work for them.

This pattern is already evident. Some schools that have been honored as high-achieving one year are finding themselves in the "needs improvement" category the next. One such school was Vandenberg Elementary in Southfield, Michigan, which President [George W.] Bush visited to promote ESEA, but which later ended up on the state's "failing" list. *USA Today* found that nineteen U.S. Department of Education Blue Ribbon exemplary schools, which had been honored after an evaluation of their school leadership, teaching, curriculum, student achievement and parental involvement, ended up ranked as "low-performing." The Department of Education "solved" this problem of inconsistency by making test scores the criterion for a blue ribbon.

The "No Child Left Behind" sanctions intended to force school improvement by means such as allowing transfers, providing tutoring to a few students, and "reconstituting" schools will do the opposite. They will pit parent against teacher, parent against parent, and school against school. The law's ultimate sanctions—privatizing school management, firing staff, state takeovers, and similar measures—have no proven record of success.

Teachers will become discouraged by inaccurate assessment of their work and the lock-step curriculum they are forced to adopt. Excellent teachers working in challenging neighborhoods will be punished for their students' "failure" to attain the proficient level on the state test. Already, stories are spreading of educators leaving the profession in response to unreasonable testing and accountability provisions.

Creative Accounting?

One rationale for "No Child Left Behind" has been that it mandates standards of accountability that may work effectively for some businesses and corporations. Unfortunately, instead of accountability, "No Child Left Behind" can lead to [creative and dishonest] accounting as schools find ways of pushing out low-scoring students to boost average test scores. For example, a school that drastically reduces the number of days of absence from school that a student is allowed before being expelled might push out enough low-scoring students to increase test averages. Moreover, students with low prospects for passing the test may be encouraged or coerced to withdraw from school. As a result, the new federal law could leave the ideal of universal high school graduation far behind.

In addition to the other flaws in the law, the federal government has failed to adequately fund ESEA mandates. Most states are now cutting budgets to the bone, watching their education resources dwindle just as they are hit with the expensive demands of the law.

In addition, neither federal nor state governments are addressing the deepening poverty that makes it difficult for so many children to learn. An impoverished environment limits the ability to succeed in school in multiple ways. Poor children move more frequently, and research shows that mobility undermines achievement. Low-income children suffer more medical and dental problems, which harms their schoolwork, yet they are less likely to have medical or dental care. Poor children have less access to non-school sources of academic forms of learning, such as museums, or high-quality after-school or summer programs. Research shows that middle and upper-income children make academic gains in the summer but poor kids actually lose ground, a major source of the achievement gap.

To some extent, schools can address these gaps with more resources, such as through high-quality after-school and summer programs that reinforce academics while also providing other valuable and fun activities. However, society needs to address issues such as adequate housing and medical care so that these cease to be major obstacles to children's success in school.

Genuine Reform

What would really help primary and secondary school children?

• The federal law should be transformed from one that uses punishments to control schools to one that supports teachers and students; from one that relies primarily on standardized tests to one that encourages high-quality assessments. Elected representatives should listen to educators and parents to determine the real needs of schools. Congress should work with the states to ensure that all schools are adequately funded and that all children have the food, housing, and medical care necessary to their success in school.

• In the short term, Congress should amend ESEA to stop the destructive inflexibility of the "adequate yearly progress" provisions and eliminate the requirement for states to annually assess all students in grades three to eight in reading and math. The amount of required standardized testing should be reduced and the draconian penalties removed. Congress must appropriate the full amount authorized for all of ESEA. The importance of all subjects necessary to a well-rounded education should be emphasized—but not by adding standardized tests in more subjects.

• Fair and accurate assessment is an important part of education. A helpful accountability system would emphasize local, classroom-based student assessment information combined with limited standardized testing. Maine and Nebraska, for example, are developing state systems that mix occasional standardized testing with local assessments, which include classroom-based assessments, such as portfolios. A helpful accountability system would be one in which each school would report its progress and problems to its own community and discuss with key constituencies how to improve the schools. Test scores should be one, rather small, part of that information. This approach would improve education and strengthen democracy. Each school would also produce an opportunity-to-learn index, including such factors as per-pupil funding, class size, number of books in libraries, teacher qualifications, and school climate and satisfaction surveys. Where schools have adequate resources but fail to provide a good education, the district or state should carefully evaluate what is wrong and intervene with methods that have been shown to succeed. Closing a neighborhood school should not be an option.

*"Schools full of poor kids can be excellent.
A few mold-breaking institutions prove
they can."*

Schools Serving the Poor Need to Emphasize Responsibility and Discipline

Scott Walter

In the viewpoint that follows, free-lance writer Scott Walter maintains that schools attended by the poor can increase academic achievement by encouraging personal responsibility and by enforcing discipline. A poor school district in New York had greatly improved test scores after an administrator required more teacher training and more weekend homework, Walter points out. Moreover, he reports, a Chicago public school in a poor neighborhood now has high test scores and high attendance rates because it is run with military-style discipline.

As you read, consider the following questions:

1. By how many percentage points did the Mount Vernon, New York, school district improve its fourth-grade English test scores between 1999 and 2001?
2. In Walter's opinion, what reforms do liberal officials fear will result from the push for objective educational standards?
3. How was Lavin Curry's life improved after he began attending a military high school, according to the author?

Nobody admits it, but the real dispute in public education today is whether schools full of poor kids can be excellent. A few mold-breaking institutions prove they can, but it requires a departure from the liberal orthodoxies of today's public-school bureaucracies.

A recent *Washington Post* story reports that Ronald Ross, superintendent in Mount Vernon, New York, one of the state's poorest and worst-performing school districts, has dramatically improved fourth-graders' test scores in just three years. In 1999, only 35 percent of Mount Vernon's public-school fourth-graders met state test standards in English; in 2001, a whopping 74 percent passed, "a rate rivaling those of many of New York's wealthiest school districts." In math, the passing rate rocketed from 51 percent to 79 percent.

Simple Changes

The simple changes Ross made in the city's elementary schools included:

- assigning each school an assistant principal and a nurse in order to free principals "to focus on instruction"
- giving free bicycles donated by local merchants to students who read 50 or more books a year
- giving teachers "more training and weekly planning sessions" with reading specialists and administrators
- giving fourth-graders "weekend homework modeled on the standardized tests."

If these mild correctives caused English scores to rise 111 percent in three years, then imagine the potential in other schools across the country.

Yet the *Post* reports all this progress with frightened claims that "top school officials worry" the new federal education law "takes a good thing—testing and accountability—too far." You see, objective standards and accountability could encourage reactionary reforms like back-to-basics curricula, firm discipline, and renewed emphasis on personal responsibility.

Another Success Story

Consider another education success story printed elsewhere in the same day's *Post:* A Chicago public high school in a bad neighborhood "has one of the highest attendance rates, one of the lowest chronic truancy rates, and some of the highest standardized test scores" in the city. Its secret? Though public it is run as a military school, and uses the Army's Junior ROTC program to help teach kids and form them into decent citizens.

High Standards

Vanderbilt University researchers studied the success of 227 schools operated by the Pentagon to serve 112,000 military kids who live on bases in the United States and abroad. The 1998 National Assessment of Educational Progress revealed high achievement levels among students at those schools, particularly among minority students. Success factors . . . included high standards and accountability through drilling and testing.

In another report, 14 Advantage charter schools showed strong academic improvements among predominantly black and Latino students from low-income homes. Those schools emphasize rigorous academic standards, an orderly learning environment, and traditional, direct instruction in reading, writing, spelling and mathematics.

Marvin Olasky, *Conservative Chronicle*, March 20, 2002.

The *Post* reports outrage over plans to replicate this successful school in a black suburb of Washington, D.C. One local politician objects that "putting a military school in a poor, black community makes it too inviting for these youngsters to go out and volunteer for the military." Worse, "staff members at the school say they were not consulted enough before the decision was made."

The school in Chicago "heard the same complaints" from the school establishment, but local backers forced the program through in an effort to save students like Lavin Curry. When he arrived at the military high school, Curry "couldn't live with his mother," had "never met his father," and was nearly expelled after he came in drunk one morning and "passed out in a school bathroom." But gradually "he realized that his teachers had simply been trying to give him what he needed: Some order in his life."

"They changed my life," he says. "They fought for me to

stay in school. They really cared about me." Now he doesn't drink or smoke, earns A's and B's, plays chess and football, has a part-time job, and has "begun talking about college, maybe even law school." He's also noticed another benefit of military school: "I don't have to worry about somebody jumping me in the hallways." Nor do the benefits stop at the schoolhouse door: "I feel proud when I go out in my uniform. There's something about wearing it. You carry yourself differently."

Now if only the politicians, bureaucrats, and pundits who insist on warehousing poor kids in conventional public schools would think differently about what Curry and his peers are capable of achieving.

"A large number of children from poor families aren't getting the basics they need."

Schools Serving the Poor Need Increased Federal Funding

Robert B. Reich

The U.S. economic crisis has led the government to cut funding to public schools, and these cuts have the most damaging effect on school districts populated by the poor, Robert B. Reich explains in the following viewpoint. While recent legislation supposedly ensures that districts will receive extra funding to assist disadvantaged and nonachieving students, federal assistance is likely to decrease as the government incurs more debt, Reich points out. Cutting funding for schools—especially those in poor districts—undermines student learning and future productivity. The federal government should dramatically increase funding to poor schools to protect America's economic future, he concludes. Reich, an economist, was U.S. Secretary of Labor from 1993 to 1997.

As you read, consider the following questions:

1. What are the dangers of high-stakes testing, in Reich's opinion?
2. What is Title I, according to the author?
3. What is the only truly American asset, in Reich's view?

Robert B. Reich, "The Real Supply Side," *The American Prospect*, vol. 14, October 2003, p. 40. Copyright © 2003 by The American Prospect, Inc. All rights reserved. Reproduced with permission from *The American Prospect*, 5 Broad St., Boston, MA 02109.

It's no secret that the nation's public schools are confronting their worst budget crisis in decades. Blame it on the combination of a lousy economy, state and local budget cuts, and unfunded federal mandates. The result is that many of America's 50 million public-school kids are going back to overcrowded classrooms, older and rattier textbooks, meager school supplies, fewer school libraries, less school sports and arts, and canceled after-school programs. Teachers are being laid off all over the country. Here in Boston, for example, five public schools have recently been closed and 400 teachers let go.

America's school budget crisis couldn't come at a worse time. The No Child Left Behind Act is just kicking in. It uses standardized tests to hold schools accountable for student achievement. If any poor racial or demographic group fails to advance for two consecutive years, the school has to offer tutoring and give parents the option of transferring their kids to a higher-scoring school.

We can debate whether this sort of accountability is a good idea. The danger with high-stakes testing, of course, is that schools become test-taking factories in which the only thing taught or learned is how to take high-stakes tests.

Yet this isn't a one-size-fits-all economy anymore; mass-production jobs are going the way of the family farm. If young people are to grow into successful adults in this new economy, they'll have to learn how to think in a variety of ways, solve new problems and become quick learners in unfamiliar situations.

Poor Children Are Left Behind

What's beyond debate, however, is the fact that a large number of children from poor families aren't getting the basics they need. Poverty is becoming ever more geographically concentrated, with the result being that local school districts in poor areas don't have nearly the revenues to counterbalance the compounding negative consequences of having a lot of poor kids together in the same schools. Title 1, the federal program designed to provide additional funding for poor districts, is woefully behind this perilous trend line.

Not even the No Child Left Behind Act is getting adequate federal funding. In order for millions of disadvantaged children to pass standardized tests, schools need extra resources to help them along. And schools that fail need extra funding for the mandated tutoring, plus the added costs of transporting students to other schools. But the federal government isn't coming up with nearly as much money as it promised when the act was passed. So far, federal appropriations are almost a third less than what was authorized, about $6 billion under the mark. As a result, a lot of the act's cost is falling on the states and cities, which can't possibly afford it.

The School-Community Connection

High academic standards, aligned tests, clear incentives and strong professional development are important, but they're not sufficient to meet the lofty goal of educating all children.

Largely ignored in this debate, and early implementation of the [No Child Left Behind] Act, are the highly visible, morally troubling, increasingly savage inequalities experienced by far too many poor children in predominantly minority urban schools, as well as in under-served, under-resourced rural schools, and their respective communities. The school-community connection is evident in the relationship between the multiple interrelated plagues: poverty, violence, ill health, broken families, unemployment, and drug and alcohol abuse—and academic failure.

Ira Harkavy and Martin Blank, *Poverty and Race*, September/October 2002.

The federal government, remember, is deep in the red. [The] deficit [for 2004] is already approaching a record $500 billion. The heart of George W. Bush's domestic policy is his $1.7 trillion in tax cuts, which, as we know by now, go mostly to wealthy families. No reputable economist believes they will stimulate the economy, for the obvious reason that rich families already spend what they want to spend. That's the very definition of being rich. The only conceivable justification for these tax cuts goes under the rubric of "supply-side economics." The theory is that the rich will invest the extra money they get from the tax cuts in new factories and equipment, thereby growing the American economy. The fallacy here is that we're in a global economy, and the money the rich save by not paying taxes is as likely to go to East Asia or Europe in search of high returns as it is to America.

What About Human Capital?

The only asset that's truly American, and likely to stay right here, is our people. I'm referring specifically to their capacity to be productive in the future because they have the education and knowledge they need. This is why skimping on our schools is bad, not just for the kids who now get stuck in larger classrooms with fewer teachers but also for the future of the American economy.

I'm not one to get bent out of shape about deficits, especially when the economy has so much underutilized capacity. But it makes absolutely no sense to give tax benefits to people at the top and simultaneously fail to fund our schools. State and local budgets are tight mainly because the economy is still struggling to break out of recession, and because states and cities don't have adequate revenues. Poor districts are especially strapped because their own tax bases have shriveled. Federal funding for poor schools needs to be dramatically expanded. The No Child Left Behind Act requires a lot more money behind it.

It's a simple lesson the Bush administration and the Republican Congress should have learned by now: The real supply side lies not with financial capital but with human capital.

Periodical Bibliography

The following articles have been selected to supplement the diverse views presented in this chapter.

Sandy Banks	"The Excessive-Homework Backlash," *Los Angeles Times*, May 21, 2002.
Irving H. Buchen	"Education in America: The Next Twenty-Five Years," *Futurist*, January/February 2003.
Catherine Cornbleth	"What Constitutes Meaningful Social Studies Teaching?" *Social Education*, April 2002.
Michael A. Fletcher	"When Good Students Can't Graduate," *Washington Post National Weekly Edition*, June 9–15, 2003.
Tamara Henry	"Math Progress Hard to Figure; Math Majors Gain Better Class Results," *USA Today*, August 6, 2001.
Caroline M. Hoxby	"Conversion of a Standardized Test Skeptic," *Reason*, August 2001.
Kay S. Hymowitz	"Anti-Social Studies," *Weekly Standard*, May 6, 2002.
Linda Jacobson	"Experts Say Young Children Need More Math," *Education Week*, September 26, 2001.
Stan Karp	"Let Them Eat Tests," *Rethinking Schools*, Summer 2002.
Daniel E. Kinnamon	"We're All Different," *Curriculum Administrator*, June 2001.
Hayes Mizell	"Achievement for Every Student," *Social Education*, January/February 2003.
William Patterson	"Breaking Out of Our Boxes," *Phi Delta Kappan*, April 2003.
Dave Posner	"Education for the Twenty-First Century," *Phi Delta Kappan*, December 2002.
Douglas B. Reeves	"Leave Me Alone and Let Me Teach!" *School Administrator*, December 2001.
Patricia J. Williams	"Tests, Tracking, and Derailment," *Nation*, April 22, 2002.

For Further Discussion

Chapter 1

1. Tom Bethell maintains that American students' relatively low test scores prove that the quality of U.S. education has deteriorated. How does Gerald W. Bracey respond to this claim? Does Bracey's viewpoint effectively refute Bethell's argument? Why or why not?

2. Roger Kimball argues that college campuses that champion "diversity" actually encourage conformity to liberal views and a rejection of conservative ideas. Patricia G. Avery contends that college campuses foster tolerance because they promote the study and discussion of diverse viewpoints—and she maintains that such an approach also benefits high school students. What evidence does each author present to support his or her conclusion? Whose argument is more persuasive? Why?

3. The authors in this chapter present several arguments describing the causes of what some consider to be a crisis in America's public schools. Compare the various viewpoints, then formulate your own appraisal of the state of public education.

Chapter 2

1. After reading the viewpoints by Clint Bolick, Barbara Miner, Alain Jehlen, David Neff, and Charles Levendosky, are you more likely—or less likely—to support the use of government funds to pay student tuitions at private or parochial schools? Defend your answer with evidence from the viewpoints.

2. Isabel Lyman and Evie Hudak have differing opinions on home schooling as an alternative to public education. What are the benefits of home education, in Lyman's view? What are the drawbacks, according to Hudak? In your opinion, do the possible benefits of home schooling outweigh the drawbacks? Why or why not?

3. Ellen Goodman argues that single-sex schools are not the answer to poor quality public education. How does Karen Stabiner respond to this argument? Which of these two viewpoints is more convincing? Explain.

Chapter 3

1. What is character education, as described by Tom Lickona, Eric Schaps, and Catherine Lewis? What reservations does Thomas J. Lasley II have about character education? Do you agree with

Lasley's view that adults must change their own behavior before they can effectively teach values to children? Explain.

2. Dennis Teti and Lewis Vaughn disagree about the proposal to display the Ten Commandments in public schools. How do the arguments of these two authors reflect differing views on the value and purpose of the Ten Commandments? Whose argument do you find more persuasive?

3. The National Science Teachers Association contends that creationism and intelligent design theory should not be covered in science courses. Patrick Glynn maintains that the exclusion of alternative theories about the development of life stifles educational debate. In each viewpoint, try to find two supporting arguments that you personally agree with. Why do you agree with them?

Chapter 4

1. Don W. Hooper and Matthew Miltich disagree about the value of standardized evaluation in education. Hooper is president of the American Association of School Administrators, while Miltich is a college-level English instructor. In what way does knowing the backgrounds of these two authors influence your assessment of their arguments? Explain your answer.

2. George W. Bush maintains that the No Child Left Behind Act will greatly improve U.S. student performance. He uses an anecdotal example about the progress of students in a predominantly low-income school to help support his argument. How does Monty Neill respond to the claims posed by Bush? What methods of support does he incorporate in his viewpoint? Whose style of argument do you find more compelling?

3. The viewpoints in this chapter include several recommendations for improving public education. Consider each recommendation and then list arguments for and against each one. Note whether the arguments are based on facts, values, emotions, or other considerations. If you believe a recommendation should not be considered at all, explain why.

Organizations to Contact

The editors have compiled the following list of organizations concerned with the issues debated in this book. The descriptions are derived from materials provided by the organizations. All have publications or information available for interested readers. The list was compiled on the date of publication of the present volume; the information provided here may change. Be aware that many organizations take several weeks or longer to respond to inquiries, so allow as much time as possible.

Achieve, Inc.
400 N. Capitol St. NW, Suite 357, Washington, DC 20001
(202) 624-1460 • fax: (202) 624-1468
Web site: www.achieve.org

Achieve's mission is to raise student performance to world-class levels through the development and implementation of high academic standards, assessments, effective educational technology, and accountability systems. Its Web site includes articles, press releases, information on benchmarking and other initiatives as well as reports, including *All Tests Are Not Equal: Why States Need to Give High-Quality Tests.*

American Federation of Teachers (AFT)
555 New Jersey Ave. NW, Washington, DC 20001
(202) 879-4400
e-mail: online@aft.org • Web site: www.aft.org

The AFT is a labor union that represents more than 1 million teachers, school staff, higher education faculty and staff, health care professionals, and state and municipal employees. *Inside AFT*, the union's weekly newsletter, and *American Teacher*, a monthly journal, are available on the AFT Web site.

Association for Supervision and Curriculum Development (ASCD)
1703 N. Beauregard St., Alexandria, VA 22311
(800) 933-2723 • (703) 578-9600
Web site: www.ascd.org

Founded in 1943, the ASCD is an international, nonprofit, nonpartisan educational organization committed to the mission of forging covenants in teaching and fostering the success of all learners. The ASCD provides professional development in curriculum and supervision; initiates and supports activities to promote educational equity for all students; and offers state-of-the-art education information services. The association distributes a variety of journals, newsletters, books, and audio- and videotapes, including the *Journal of Curriculum and Supervision*, *Educational Leadership*, and *Education Update*.

Canadian Education Association (CEA)/Association Canadienne d'Education

317 Adelaide St. W., Suite 300, Toronto, ON M5V 1P9 Canada
(416) 591-6300 • fax: (416) 591-5345
e-mail: info@cea-ace.ca • Web site: www.acea.ca

The CEA is the only national, bilingual, not-for-profit organization promoting public education in Canada. Its publications, which include the *Newsletter/Le Bulletin*, *Education Canada* magazine, and the annual *CEA Handbook*, report on key issues, disseminate educational research, and provide practical information.

Eagle Forum

PO Box 618, Alton, IL 62002
(618) 462-5415 • fax: (618) 462-8909
e-mail: eagle@eagleforum.org • Web site: www.eagleforum.org

The Eagle Forum is an educational and political organization that advocates traditional family values. The forum promotes parental choice of schooling and religious freedom in the classroom and opposes outcome-based education. The organization offers several books and publishes the monthly newsletter *Education Reporter*.

Educational Commission of the States (ECS)

700 Broadway, #1200, Denver, CO 80203-3460
(303) 299-3600 • fax: (303) 296-8332
e-mail: ecs@ecs.org • Web site: www.ecs.org

The ECS is a national nonprofit organization that was created in 1965 to improve public education by facilitating the exchange of information, ideas, and experiences among state policy makers and education leaders. It creates opportunities to build partnerships, share information, and promote the development of policy based on available research and strategies. It publishes an annual report and *State Education Leader*, a triquarterly journal.

FairTest: National Center for Fair and Open Testing

342 Broadway, Cambridge, MA 02139
(617) 864-4810 • fax: (617) 497-2224
e-mail: info@fairtest.org • Web site: www.fairtest.org

FairTest is an advocacy group that opposes the use of standardized tests. It works to end the abuses, misuses, and flaws of standardized testing and to ensure that evaluations are accurate, relevant, and educationally sound. FairTest publishes the quarterly *FairTest Examiner* and offers fact sheets as well as a catalog of materials on K–12 and university testing.

The Heritage Foundation
214 Massachusetts Ave. NE, Washington, DC 20002-4999
(202) 546-4400 • fax: (202) 546-8328
e-mail: info@heritage.org • Web site: www.heritage.org
The foundation is a public policy research institute that advocates limited government, individual freedom, and traditional values. It supports parental school choice as a means of improving American education. The foundation publishes the quarterly *Policy Review* and other papers and monographs on such issues as multicultural-ism and discrimination in universities.

Home School Legal Defense Association (HSLDA)
PO Box 3000, Purcellville, VA 20134-9000
(540) 338-5600 • fax: (540) 338-2733
e-mail: info@hslda.org • Web site: www.hslda.org
The association is committed to protecting the rights of parents to direct the education of their children. It provides legal assistance to homeschooling families challenged by state government or local school boards. HSLDA publishes the *Home School Court Report* quarterly magazine as well as brochures about home education. Its Web site includes links to articles, reports, and dozens of national, state, and local homeschool organizations.

Institute for Creation Research (ICR)
10946 Woodside Ave. N., Santee, CA 92071
(619) 448-0900 • fax: (619) 448-3469
Web site: www.icr.org
The Institute for Creation Research Graduate School is a private not-for-profit corporation that trains students in all scientific dis-ciplines, including the teachings of scientific creationism. The ICR publishes the monthly news booklet *Acts & Facts* and *Days of Praise*, a quarterly devotional booklet. Research papers on creation science are available on its Web site.

National Association of Scholars (NAS)
221 Witherspoon St., 2nd Fl., Princeton, NJ 08542-3215
(609) 683-7878 • fax: (609) 683-0316
e-mail: nas@nas.org • Web site: www.nas.org

The National Association of Scholars is an organization of professors, graduate students, and college administrators committed to academic freedom and the free exchange of ideas in universities. It believes in a curriculum that stresses the achievements of Western civilization and opposes restrictive speech codes, racial or gender preferences for faculty and students, and an overemphasis on multiculturalism. The NAS publishes the quarterly *Academic Questions.*

National Center for Science Education (NCSE)

420 40th St., Suite 2, Oakland, CA 94609-2509
(510) 601-7203 • fax: (510) 601-7204
e-mail: ncseoffice@ncseweb.org • Web site: www.natcenscied.org

NCSE is a nonprofit organization working to defend the teaching of evolution against sectarian attack. It is a clearinghouse for information and advice to keep evolution in the science classroom and creationism out. NCSE also works to increase public understanding of evolution and science and has programs to help teachers improve their teaching of evolutionary theory. The center publishes books, pamphlets, and the bimonthly journal, *Reports of NCSE.*

National Education Association (NEA)

1201 16th St. NW, Washington, DC 20036-3290
(202) 833-4000 • fax: (202) 822-7974
Web site: www.nea.org

The NEA is America's oldest and largest volunteer-based organization dedicated to advancing the cause of public education. Its activities at the local, state, and national levels include conducting professional workshops for teachers, lobbying for needed school resources and higher educational standards, and spearheading innovative projects that reshape the learning process. Two of the NEA's publications, the monthly magazine *NEA Today* and the quarterly journal *Thought & Action*, are available on its Web site.

National Parent Teacher Association (PTA)

330 N. Wabash Ave., Suite 2100, Chicago, IL 60611
(800) 307-4782 • (312) 670-6782 • fax: (312) 670-6783
Web site: www.pta.org

The PTA is the largest volunteer child advocacy organization in the United States. A not-for-profit organization of parents, educators, students, and other citizens active in their schools and communities, the PTA works to focus national attention on the education, health, and welfare of children. Its Web site includes links to the monthly magazine *Our Children* and to a press room of archived articles and reports concerning educational issues.

Poverty and Race Research Action Council (PRRAC)
3000 Connecticut Ave. NW, Suite 200, Washington, DC 20008
(202) 387-9887 • fax: (202) 387-0764
e-mail: info@prrac.org • Web site: www.prrac.org

The Poverty and Race Research Action Council is a nonpartisan, national, not-for-profit organization convened by major civil rights, civil liberties, and antipoverty groups. PRRAC's main purpose is to link social science research to advocacy work in order to successfully address problems at the intersection of race and poverty. Its bimonthly publication, *Poverty and Race*, often includes articles on race- and income-based educational inequities in the United States.

U.S. Department of Education
600 Independence Ave. SW, Washington, DC 20202-6510
Web site: www.ed.gov

This governmental department promotes educational excellence for all Americans. It offers detailed information on educational policy and programs as well as up-to-date research and statistics on education. Its Web site includes a press room, a searchable topic index, and a comprehensive explanation of the 2001 No Child Left Behind Act.

Bibliography of Books

Jerry Aldridge and Renitta Goldman — *Current Issues and Trends in Education.* Boston: Allyn and Bacon, 2002.

Martin Bickman — *Minding American Education: Reclaiming the Tradition of Active Learning.* New York: Teachers College Press, 2003.

Bruce J. Biddle — *The Untested Accusation: Principals, Research Knowledge, and Policy Making in Schools.* Westport, CT: Ablen, 2002.

Gerald W. Bracey — *Bail Me Out: Handling Difficult Data and Tough Questions About Public Schools.* Thousand Oaks, CA: Corwin Press, 2000.

Dennis Carlson — *Leaving Safe Harbors: Toward a New Progressivism in American Education and Public Life.* New York: Routledge Falmer, 2002.

Robert W. Cole, ed. — *More Strategies for Educating Everybody's Children.* Alexandria, VA: Association for Supervision and Curriculum Development, 2001.

Kieran Egan — *Getting It Wrong from the Beginning: Our Progressivist Inheritance from Robert Spencer, John Dewey, and Jean Piaget.* New Haven, CT: Yale University Press, 2002.

Milton Gaither — *American Educational History Revisited: A Critique of Progress.* New York: Teachers College Press, 2003.

Henry A. Giroux — *The Abandoned Generation: Democracy Beyond the Culture of Fear.* New York: Palgrave Macmillan, 2003.

David T. Gordon, ed. — *A Nation Reformed? American Education Twenty Years After A Nation at Risk.* Cambridge, MA: Harvard Education Press, 2003.

E.D. Hirsch Jr., Joseph F. Kett, and James Trefil — *The New Dictionary of Cultural Literacy.* Boston: Houghton Mifflin, 2001.

James Davison Hunter — *Culture Wars: The Struggle to Control the Family, Art, Education, Law, and Politics in America.* New York: Basic Books, 2000.

Alan Charles Kors and Harvey Silvergate — *The Shadow University: The Betrayal of Liberty on America's Campuses.* New York: Free Press, 2000.

Tom Loveless, ed. — *The Great Curriculum Debate: How Should We Teach Reading and Math?* Washington, DC: Brookings Institution Press, 2001.

Jane Roland Martin	*Cultural Miseducation: In Search of a Democratic Solution.* New York: Teachers College Press, 2002.
John Merrow	*Choosing Excellence: "Good Enough" Schools Are Not Good Enough.* Lanham, MD: Scarecrow Press, 2001.
Terry M. Moe, ed.	*A Primer on America's Schools.* Stanford, CA: Hoover Institution Press, 2001.
Sarah Mondale and Sarah B. Patton, eds.	*School: The Story of American Public Education.* Boston: Beacon Press, 2001.
Donald Hugh Parkerson and Jo Ann Parkerson	*Transitions in American Education: A Social History of Teaching.* New York: Routledge Falmer, 2001.
John and Kathy Perry	*The Complete Guide to Homeschooling.* Los Angeles: Lowell House, 2000.
Paul E. Peterson, ed.	*Our Schools and Our Future: Are We Still at Risk?* Stanford, CA: Hoover Institution Press, 2003.
Douglas S. Reed	*On Equal Terms: The Constitutional Politics of Educational Opportunity.* Princeton, NJ: Princeton University Press, 2001.
J. Martin Rochester	*Class Warfare: Besieged Schools, Bewildered Parents, Betrayed Kids, and the Attack on Excellence.* San Francisco: Encounter Books, 2002.
John L. Rury	*Education and Social Change: Themes in the History of American Schooling.* Mahwah, NJ: L. Erlbaum Associates, 2002.
Peter Schrag	*Final Test: The Battle for Adequacy in America's Schools.* New York: New Press, 2003.
Mitchell L. Stevens	*Kingdom of Children: Culture and Controversy in the Homeschooling Movement.* Princeton, NJ: Princeton University Press, 2001
Tony Wagner	*Making the Grade: Reinventing America's Schools.* New York: Routledge Falmer, 2002.
Dan H. Wishnietsky	*American Education in the 21st Century.* Bloomington, IN: Phi Delta Kappa Educational Foundation, 2001.
U.S. Department of Education	*Rural Home Schooling and Place-Based Education.* Washington, DC: U.S. Department of Education, 2001.

Index